Helping Students Motivate Themselves

Practical Answers to Classroom Challenges

Larry Ferlazzo

EYE ON EDUCATION
6 DEPOT WAY WEST, SUITE 106
LARCHMONT, NY 10538
(914) 833–0551
(914) 833–0761 fax
www.eyeoneducation.com

Library of Congress Cataloging-in-Publication Data

Ferlazzo, Larry.

 Helping students motivate themselves : practical answers to classroom challenges / by Larry Ferlazzo.

    p. cm.

  ISBN 978-1-59667-181-2

 1. Motivation in education. 2. Effective teaching. 3. Classroom management. I. Title.

  LB1065.F47 2011

  371.102—dc22

                                            2011006834

10 9 8 7 6 5 4 3 2

Also Available from EYE ON EDUCATION

The Passion-Driven Classroom:
A Framework for Teaching and Learning
Angela Maiers and Amy Sandvold

Battling Boredom: 99 Strategies to Spark Student Engagement
Bryan Harris

ENGAGING Teens in Their Own Learning:
8 Keys to Student Success
Paul J. Vermette

What Great Teachers Do *Differently*: 14 Things That Matter Most
Todd Whitaker

Rigor is NOT a Four-Letter Word
Barbara R. Blackburn

Classroom Motivation from A to Z:
How to Engage Your Students in Learning
Barbara R. Blackburn

50 Ways to Improve Student Behavior:
Simple Solutions to Complex Challenges
Annette Breaux and Todd Whitaker

What Do You Say When…?
Best Practice Language for Improving Student Behavior
Hal Holloman and Peggy H. Yates

How the Best Teachers Avoid the 20 Most
Common Teaching Mistakes
Elizabeth Breaux

'Tween Crayons and Curfews: Tips for Middle School Teachers
Heather Wolpert-Gawron

Critical Thinking and Formative Assessments:
Increasing the Rigor in Your Classroom
Betsy Moore and Todd Stanley

But I'm Not a Reading Teacher:
Strategies for Literacy Instruction in the Content Areas
Amy Benjamin

Online Resources

Helping Students Motivate Themselves offers readers several online resources for further research, supplemental materials, and user involvement. For ease of access, these links have been posted on the book's product page on Eye On Education's website: **www.eyeoneducation.com**. From the home page, search by author or book title to locate the page for *Helping Students Motivate Themselves*. Then scroll to the bottom of the page and click on **Online Resources** for an index of easily clickable links.

Free Downloads

Many of the figures discussed and displayed in this book are also available on Eye On Education's website as Adobe Acrobat files. Permission has been granted to purchasers of this book to download these figures and print them.

You can access these downloads by visiting Eye On Education's website: www.eyeoneducation.com. From the home page, click on FREE, then click on Supplemental Downloads. Alternatively, you can search or browse our website to find this book, then click "Log in to Access Supplemental Downloads." Your book-buyer access code is HSM-7181-2.

Index of Free Downloads

Meet the Author

Larry Ferlazzo teaches English and Social Studies at Luther Burbank High School in Sacramento, California. He has written two previous books, *Building Parent Engagement in Schools* (with coauthor Lorie Hammond) and *English Language Learners: Teaching Strategies That Work*.

He writes a popular education blog at http://Larryferlazzo.edublogs.org and has won numerous awards, including the Leadership for a Changing World Award from the Ford Foundation. He also was the Grand Prize Winner of the International Reading Association Award for Technology and Reading and was given The Education Partnership Award by the College of Education at California State University, Sacramento.

His articles on education policy appear regularly in the *Washington Post*, *Teacher Magazine*, and *The Huffington Post*. In addition, his work has appeared in publications such as *The New York Times*, *Educational Leadership*, *Social Policy*, and *Language Magazine*.

Larry was a community organizer for nineteen years prior to becoming a public school teacher.

He is married and has three children and two grandchildren.

Acknowledgements

I'd like to thank my family—Stacia, Rich, Shea, Ava, Nik, Karli, and, especially, my wife, Jan—for their support. In addition, I need to express my appreciation to Kelly Young at Pebble Creek Labs and my colleagues at Luther Burbank High School, including Katie Hull Sypnieski and Principal Ted Appel, and many other teachers there who have taught the lessons you'll find in this book and improved upon them. Last, but certainly not least, a big thank you goes to Burbank students, from whom I have learned so much.

Contents

Introduction

This book comes out of my seven years of teaching at Luther Burbank High School in Sacramento, California, and out of my previous nineteen years working as a community organizer.

It comes out of my recognizing that for me to be as effective as I wanted to be as a teacher, I needed to identify ways that I could help my students both learn content knowledge and develop higher-order thinking skills and the attributes that good community leaders must have, including self-motivation, personal responsibility, and perseverance. Increasingly, research shows that these qualities are critical for success in careers, college, and in life (Hampel, 2010). In fact, a 2011 review of more than 200 studies covering nearly 300,000 students found that simple lessons taught by teachers covering these kinds of topics resulted in substantial student academic gains (Sparks, 2011).

And this book comes out of my understanding that developing these kinds of attributes needs to be done in conjunction with students gaining the academic skills they need to learn. In most of our schools today, for better or worse, both teachers and their students are primarily held accountable for teaching and learning academic skills—no matter how important we believe other life skills might be.

This book shares classroom-tested strategies to accomplish both goals simultaneously.

Most, although not all, chapters follow a similar structure. They begin with a question relating to a common classroom problem, which is followed by an imaginary complaint/concern voiced by a teacher. Even though it is "imaginary," I'd bet most of us have either said or thought something like each concern at some point during our teaching career.

Next is a section on immediate responses that teachers can take *today* to deal with the issue. Each response is accompanied by research supporting it. Almost all of the suggestions support developing higher-order thinking skills and enhancing self-motivation, personal responsibility, and perseverance. However, there are a few ideas sprinkled throughout the book that, while not necessarily designed to further those specific qualities, don't undermine them either—I have just found these ideas to be effective. As Ralph Waldo Emerson wrote in "Self-Reliance": "A foolish consistency is the hobgoblin of little minds…" (Emerson, n.d.).

A "Setting the Stage" section comes next and provides ideas (and supporting research) on what teachers can do to provide longer-term solutions.

The final section of each chapter includes detailed lesson plans, including reproducible plans, to implement some of the "Setting the Stage" recommendations. Each lesson plan includes the *Common Core Anchor State Standards for English Language Arts, Grades 6–12* ("The Standards," 2010) that are covered by the lesson. A webpage containing all Internet links for use with these lessons can be found both at my blog (http://larryferlazzo.edublogs.org/) and at the Eye On Education website (http://www.eyeoneducation.com/).

The lessons have specific suggestions for incorporating technology into the activities. Even though each lesson has a different technology suggestion, most of the suggestions are appropriate for all of the lessons in the book. Those ideas, along with the activities recommended in the free-standing chapter on using technology in the classroom in Question 12, provide a wealth of different ways to effectively use technology to enhance student learning.

This book is not designed as a road map; rather, it should serve as a compass to point us and our students in the right direction.

Part I

Classroom Culture

How Do You Motivate Students?

I work so hard at trying to get these kids motivated. Some are, but so many aren't. They just seem to want to get by—if that. I try to encourage them—I'm their biggest cheerleader! But it can get so tiring. I feel like I'm pushing a rope with some of my students. Why can't they just want to achieve instead of having to be pushed into it?

Strategies that teachers will often use in efforts to motivate students include offering incentives and rewards—"If you read a certain number of books you'll get a prize!"—or cheerlead relentlessly—"Good job, Karen!" It's also not unusual for teachers to just "give up" on some students, "They just don't want to learn!"

One lesson community organizers learn is that you might be able to threaten, cajole, badger, or bribe someone to do something over the short-term, but getting someone to do something beyond a very, very short time-frame is a radically different story.

Organizers believe that you cannot really motivate anybody else. However, you *can* help people discover what they can use to motivate themselves.

This is very similar to what Edward Deci, one of the premier researchers and authorities on intrinsic motivation, wrote, "The proper question is not, 'how can people motivate others?' but rather, 'how can people create the conditions within which others will motivate themselves?'" (Deci, 1995, p. 10). In fact, this perspective is in keeping with the original word roots of *motivation*. It comes from *motive*, which, in the fifteenth century, meant "that which inwardly moves a person to behave a certain way" ("Motive," n.d.).

When we are trying to motivate students—often unsuccessfully—the energy is coming from *us*. When we help students discover their own motivation, and challenge them to act on it, more of the energy is coming from *them*.

Community organizers call it the difference between *irritation*—pushing people to do something *you* want them to do—and *agitation*—challenging them to act on something *they* have identified as important in their lives.

This chapter first briefly reviews research that demonstrates the long-term dangers of the incentives and rewards system many of us use to "motivate" our students. Next, a few strategies are discussed that a teacher can immediately implement in the classroom to help students find their inner motivation. Finally, the chapter ends by identifying ways to "set the stage" and help students identify more sources of intrinsic motivation.

Four detailed lesson plans and related reproducibles are included.

The Dangers of Incentives and Rewards

Many studies show that—contrary to what many of us believe—providing rewards to induce desired behaviors can result in long-term damage to intrinsic motivation. As Daniel Pink states in his book, *Drive* (2009, p. 8), "Rewards can deliver a short-term boost—just as a jolt of caffeine can keep you cranking for a few more hours. But the effect wears off—and, worse, can reduce a person's longer-term motivation to continue the project."

Researchers believe this loss of intrinsic motivation happens because contingent rewards—if you do this, then you'll get that—force people to give up some of their autonomy (Pink, 2009, p. 38). Deci (1995, p. 2), Pink, and William Glasser (Van Tassell, 2004) all highlight this need for learner autonomy as crucial for students and for all of us. As economist Russ Roberts (2010) commented in an interview with Pink, "Nobody wants to feel like a rat in maze."

Rewards (and punishments) are effective, however, in getting people to do mechanical and routine work that can be accomplished simply. For example, they can result in employees working faster on an assembly line or in getting students to make basic changes in their behavior in the classroom. However, rewards can be destructive in advancing anything that requires higher-order thinking (Pink, 2009, p. 46). Question 4: How Do You Regain

Control of an Out-Of-Control Class? recounts what both of these types of results can look like in the classroom.

Of course, we all expect and need what Pink calls "baseline rewards" (Pink, 2009, p. 35). These are the basics of adequate "compensation." At school, these might include students expecting fair grading, a caring teacher who works to provide fairly engaging lessons, a clean classroom. Pink writes:

> If someone's baseline rewards aren't adequate or equitable, her focus will be on the unfairness of her situation and the anxiety of her circumstance. You'll get neither the predictability of extrinsic motivation nor the weirdness of intrinsic motivation. You'll get very little motivation at all. But once we're past that threshold, carrots and sticks can achieve precisely the opposite of their intended aims. (Pink, 2009, p. 35)

None of these points mean that students cannot be recognized and celebrated for their success. The key is to not hold it out as a "carrot" but, instead, to provide it as an unexpected "bonus" (Chai, 2009).

The word "incentives" comes from *incendere*, which means "to kindle." The dictionary says that "to kindle" means "to start a fire burning." The idea is not to tell students that they will die from the cold or from being eaten by wolves if they do not start a fire *right now* and *right here* and in *this way*. Nor is the idea to say that, if they do what we tell them, they will get an extra bag of marshmallows to toast. Instead, the goal can be to find out where they want to set their fire and why, and perhaps help them learn how to use matches or a flint, and give them advice on the best place to find some dry wood.

This chapter provides ideas on how to help students "incentivize" themselves. Although this is not the primary intent of the ideas listed here, one study has found that it can even be helpful for people to literally "bribe" *themselves* with rewards if they meet their goals (Kristof, 2009). This can be applied in the classroom by suggesting that students list how they can reward themselves—a night of video games, sleeping in late—if they achieve some of their goals.

Immediate Actions

Praise Effort and Specific Actions

If we only praise students in general—"You're very smart"—many will then try to avoid taking risks and stretching themselves. They will focus more on maintaining their image and believe that they will embarrass themselves by making mistakes. Praising effort—"You worked really hard today"— or praising specific actions—"Your topic sentence communicates the main idea"—can make students feel that they are more in control of their success, and that their doing well is less dependent on their "natural intelligence" (Bronson, 2007). Question 5: How Do You Help Students See Problems as Opportunities, Not Frustrations? provides more information on this topic.

Build Relationships

Teachers building relationships with their students by showing that they care about them, and by learning about their lives, dreams, and challenges, are key to helping students motivate themselves. Dr. Jami Jones (2010) and others (e.g., Posnick-Goodwin, 2010) have shown that caring relationships with teachers can help build resiliency (the capacity to persevere and overcome challenges) among children. By learning about student interests, teachers can also help connect what is being taught in the classroom to students' lives and discover their short- and long-term goals.

As William Glasser (1988, p. 21) and others have found, many students "will not work to learn" unless they see how lessons can help them with their short- or long-term goals. More information on how to build those relationships can be found in Question 3: How Do You Deal With a Student Who Is Being Disruptive in Class?

Use Cooperative Learning

Teaching engaging lessons is a "baseline reward" expectation of students. Boring lessons will not help students to develop their intrinsic motivation to learn. That does not mean, however, that teachers have to put on costumes and become entertainers. It can, however, suggest that teachers consider keeping lecturing to a minimum and, instead, use many of the teaching strategies that have been found to be more effective for student learning. Most of these methods include some sort of cooperative learning (Saville, 2009). These can be as basic as "think-pair-share" or as ambitious as problem-based learning or project-based learning. More information on how to implement these strategies in the classroom is found in Question 12: What Are the Easiest Ways to Use Educational Technology in the Classroom?

Show Students the Economic and Health Advantages of Doing Well in School

Multiple studies show a wide income disparity based on educational attainment. For example, according to the U.S. Census Bureau, adults with advanced degrees earn four times the salary of those with less than a high school degree (U.S. Census Bureau, 2009). There are similar differences between the likely length someone will be unemployed (U.S. College Search, 2010), one's overall health ("Poor Face Greater Health Burden," 2009), and even how long people will live (Hull, 2010). Studies show that just showing students this kind of information can result in students being more motivated to learn (Jacobs, 2010). A collection of this kind of data can be found at http://larryferlazzo.edublogs.org/2010/09/15/a-collection-of-the-best-lists-on-encouraging-students-to-attend-college/.

Creating Opportunities for Students to Help Make Decisions

People are more motivated and confident when they believe they have more control over their environment. "People with low-power mindsets do less than they otherwise could," said one motivation researcher (Rigoglioso, 2008). Inviting students to have a voice in classroom decisions—where they sit, what day a test takes place, in what order units are studied, or even where a plant should be placed in the classroom—can help them develop that greater sense of control. An added benefit to this strategy could be fewer discipline issues. William Glasser suggests that power is a key need of students, and that 95% of classroom management problems happen because students are trying to fulfill that need (Ryan & Cooper, 2008, p. 85).

Setting the Stage

The Brain Is Like a Muscle

Students' learning that intelligence is not fixed at a certain level and that they can actually "grow" their brain by learning has been shown to help develop intrinsic motivation in students. Carol Dweck (2008), a leading researcher in this area, calls it the difference between a "growth mindset" and a "fixed mindset." Those who understand that their ability will grow as they work harder, and that their brain cells will actually physically grow the more they learn, are more focused on learning and are more resilient. After using "The Brain is Like a Muscle" Lesson Plan (see page 14), a teacher can regularly remind students of this understanding verbally and through leaving student-created posters on the wall.

Setting Goals

Students setting their own goals can help channel their focus and help them assess their progress and make the necessary changes to accomplish them. Goal-setting (Siegle, 2000) can result in increased student motivation and achievement (Ormand, 2008). Although it is important for learner autonomy that students actually decide on their goals, teachers may need to provide some guidance on what realistic expectations might be, especially if some goals relate to a numerical advance on a formal assessment. For example, teachers could share with students the "average" growth that students make during the year in regular formative assessments, and the scores necessary to advance to different levels in state standardized tests.

In addition to those kinds of obvious academic achievement goals, the Northwest Regional Education Laboratory has identified several important characteristics of a self-directed learner that students could consider as qualities that might want to improve in themselves. These include intrinsic motivation, self-control, taking personal responsibility, metacognition/reflection, and being goal-oriented (Northwest Regional Educational Laboratory, 2004). The Goal-Setting Lesson Plan (see page 19) includes a discussion of these qualities, and a detailed process to introduce students to the idea of setting goals.

In fact, it can be important to place more of an emphasis on "learning goals" like developing these qualities, or ones like wanting to be more disciplined about reading for a half-hour each night or wanting to work to work better in groups by encouraging everyone to speak, than on "academic performance goals." Studies show that students who focus more on learning goals actually improved more on their G.P.A. than those who emphasized wanting to improve their grades (Latham & Locke, 2006, p. 334). A review of 100 studies found that "…students who focused too heavily on performance ironically performed less well academically, thought less critically, and had a harder time overcoming failure" (Viadero, 2010).

This idea is similar to how community organizers operate. Organizing groups are often more effective in building affordable housing than groups that solely focus on affordable housing development. They also tend to be more successful in getting people into jobs that pay a living wage with benefits than graduates of traditional training agencies. The primary reason for that success is that good organizers are focused on helping people learn to become leaders, and then use housing and jobs campaigns as tools to help people develop leadership skills (which include many of the same characteristics of a self-directed learner). The idea is to help people become life-long learners, after which the performance outcomes will come.

There are six other important points to keep in mind when doing goal-setting with students.

Reviewing Goals Regularly

It is not a matter of doing the Goal-Setting Lesson Plan (see page 19) once and forgetting about it the rest of the year. Rather, students could complete a semester goal form (Figure 1.1).

They could then use that as a guide to complete their weekly goal forms (Figure 1.2, page 10). Each weekly goal does not necessarily have to correlate with a semester goal, but it provides some guidance. And, of course, students can change their goals.

Figure 1.1. Semester Goal Form

Your name: _____

Semester Goal Sheet

The end of the first semester is in January. Please think about your performance and your learning goals for the rest of the semester and complete this sheet. I will make a copy of this sheet and return it to you tomorrow. If you get it signed by your parent/ guardian, you will receive extra credit.

Performance Goals

Grade

- ♦ What is your percentage and grade in this class now? _____
- ♦ What percentage and grade do you want at the end of the semester? _____

Reading Scores

- ♦ What is your fluency score now? _____
- ♦ What do you want your fluency score to be at the end of the semester? _____
- ♦ What is your cloze score now? _____
- ♦ What do you want your cloze score to be at the end of the semester? _____

Number of Books Read

- ♦ How many books have you read so far this semester? _____
- ♦ How many books do you want to finish by the end of the semester? _____

Learning Goals

What other goals do you have for yourself (a more positive attitude, read more challenging books, take more leadership in the class, be more organized, etc.)?

1.

2.

3.

Three things you are going to do each week to accomplish your goals:

1.

2.

3.

_____
Parent Signature

Figure 1.2. Weekly Goal Sheet

GOAL SHEET

Name _____ Date _____

Current Grade in Class _____

Goal _____

_____

Method for Achievement _____

_____

I rate my work in this class last week as a

    1   2   3   4   5   6   7   8   9   10

Last Week's Goal _____

Achieved? _____ Why or Why not? _____

Parent/ Guardian Response

Printed Name _____

Current Contact Information _____

_____

Questions/Comments _____

_____

_____

Signature _____

(Developed by Rachel Schultz. Reprinted with permission.)

Partner Support

It can be very useful to have students identify partners to support them in their efforts to achieve their goals. Studies documenting people achieving success in developing spending goals (Kristof, 2009) and exercise goals (Helliker, 2010) found that the emotional support provided by partners can improve the probability of success. After identifying goals, students can choose "buddies" for the semester, and, after modeling for students what a good "conference" might look like, teachers could have them meet once each week for a few minutes to do two things:

1. Share your goal for that week. Did you achieve it? If you did, what helped you do it? If you didn't, what can you do differently?

2. Provide positive feedback and helpful suggestions to your partner.

Asking Questions

An important study found that how we frame goals can have an impact on whether we achieve them or not. It suggests that instead of just listing the goal, we should first ask ourselves if we can achieve it ("Will We Succeed," 2010). In other words, instead of writing or saying "My goal is to understand the Pythagorean Theorem this week," students should write:

Can I understand the Pythagorean Theorem this week?

Yes, I can understand the Pythagorean Theorem this week!

Asking the question, and then responding, requires a stronger affirmation and commitment than just listing the goal.

Making Goals Public

Making goals public can help increase the chances of success (DiSalvo, 2010, January 10). This could be optional for students, but there may be times when teachers might want to strongly encourage them to make their goals public. For example, near the end of the school year, teachers could ask students to answer these questions and make them into illustrated posters:

What are three things you can do to help you finish the school year strong academically?

What is one thing you can do to help your classmates finish the year strong academically?

The posters could be placed on the walls, and periodically students could walk around to review them. Having them see the posters during a challenging time of the year can function as a reminder to them—and as a reminder to teachers to remind them—to stay focused.

Designing Action Plans

Peter Drucker wrote "The best plan is only…good intentions unless it degenerates into work" (Drucker, 1974, p. 128). In addition to spending time helping students determine their goals, teachers also need to help them design realistic plans to achieve them. The more specific the plan, the likelier the success in achieving them (Ferlazzo, 2010). Teachers showing examples is one way to do this. Demonstrating it through the instructional method of "concept attainment" is an excellent way to illustrate examples for both action plans and the goals themselves.

Concept attainment is a form of *inductive* learning. In inductive learning, students use given examples to construct a pattern and form a concept or rule. In contrast, in *deductive* learning the concept or rule is given first and then students practice applying it.

A teacher could use concept attainment to help students develop effective plans by using a sheet like the one pictured in Figure 1.3.

After placing it on an overhead projector or document camera, the teacher would cover everything other than the "Yes" and "No" titles. The teacher would say that he is going to show examples of effective action plans under "Yes" and not-so-effective action plans under "No." He would explain that he wants students to try to figure out why some are under "Yes" and others are under "No." He would then show and read the first item under "Yes" and then show the first item under "No." He could ask students to "think-pair-share" to determine the difference and ask for responses. He would continue with that process until students discovered that specificity was the key difference. At that point, he could ask students to correct the "No" examples and also come up additional "Yes" ones.

The instructional method of concept attainment can be applied effectively to many different types of lessons in all subjects.

Getting Enough Sleep

One reason some students do not appear very motivated to learn might be because they do not get enough sleep and are tired at school. Teens are physically "wired" to go to sleep later and wake-up later ("Teens and Sleep Patterns," n.d.). Because of that, some schools are starting at a later time in the morning ("Delayed School Start Time," 2010).Given that this change is unlikely to occur in many districts, helping students become more aware of the negative consequence of not getting enough rest could help motivate them to change their sleeping habits. The "Why We Should Sleep More" Lesson Plan (see page 23) helps student learn that a lack of sleep leads to weight gain, lower grade, and increased levels of depression. Because of additional stress in the lives of lower-income children, they are at an even higher risk for these negative consequences ("Poor Children More Vulnerable," 2010).

Figure 1.3. Concept Attainment: Action Plans to Achieve Goals

Yes	No
To make sure I have time to read at night, I will set the alarm clock to remind me to stop playing video games.	
	I will work harder.
I don't want to get any referrals to the office this year, so when I feel like I'm getting real angry I'll ask for a pass to the restroom so I can cool off.	
	I'll get less angry.
I want to stop blaming others for my mistakes, so I'll put a sticky note on my desk each day saying "Take Responsibility" to remind me.	
	I'll try to remember that it's not always someone else's fault.
I want to work better in small groups, so every time we have them I'll assume my job is to make sure everybody participates.	
	I'll try to take more leadership when we work in small groups.

Studies have found that lack of exposure to "morning light" exacerbates teen's difficulty in getting to sleep earlier. They miss much of this light because they often travel to school so early and spend the day inside ("Lack of Morning Light," 2010). Keeping classroom shade/drapes open and windows uncovered could help mitigate this effect.

Recognizing That What Is Being Learned Is Useful

The importance of students seeing that what they are learning will help them with their short- and long-term goals was discussed earlier in the "Build Relationships" section (see page 6). By getting to know students and their hopes and dreams, teachers will be able to more explicitly connect lessons to students' lives. Helping people see the significance and meaning of what they are doing can increase intrinsic motivation (Pink, 2011). In addition to teachers doing the connecting, it can also be useful to have students themselves identify how what they are learning is meaningful for their lives.

The Helping in the Future Lesson Plan (see page 27) serves this purpose. Using another example of inductive learning, students identify how what they are learning can benefit them in the future. The categorization methods involved in using "data sets" (which is the primary material in this lesson) have been regularly shown to develop and strengthen higher-order thinking skills (Ferlazzo, 2010, p. 78). Like concept attainment, data sets can be used in various lessons across the curriculum.

"The Brain Is Like a Muscle" Lesson Plan

Instructional Objectives

Students will:

1. Learn that they can physically "grow" their brain through the effort of learning new things.

2. Be able to explain what happens to their brain when they learn new things.

Duration

One 55-minute class period

Common Core English Language Arts Standards

Reading:

1. Read closely to determine what the text says explicitly and to make logical inferences from it; cite specific textual evidence when writing or speaking to support conclusions drawn from the text.

2. Determine central ideas or themes of a text and analyze their development; summarize the key supporting details and ideas.

3. Read and comprehend complex literary and informational texts independently and proficiently.

Writing:

1. Write arguments to support claims in an analysis of substantive topics or texts, using valid reasoning and relevant and sufficient evidence.

Speaking & Listening:

1. Prepare for and participate effectively in a range of conversations and collaborations with diverse partners, building on others' ideas and expressing their own clearly and persuasively.

Language:

1. Demonstrate command of the conventions of standard English grammar and usage when writing or speaking.

2. Demonstrate command of the conventions of standard English capitalization, punctuation, and spelling when writing.

Materials:

1. Copies of the four-page hand-out from Brainology, "You Can Grow Your Intelligence" (http://www.brainology.us/websitemedia/youcangrowy ourintelligence.pdf), for every student.

2. Computer projector and computer access to show one short video showing neurons growing (search on the Internet for "neurons and how they work" and choose any that are accessible).

Procedure

First Day

1. Teachers writes the following on a whiteboard or shows on an overhead:

   Option One:

   ♦ Yes, I think the brain is like a muscle and the more you exercise it, the stronger it gets.

   Option Two:

   ♦ You are born with being however smart or dumb you are and that's the way it is.

2. Teacher asks students to write down which one they agree with and why. Students share their response with a partner, and the teacher asks specific students to share with the entire class.

3. Teacher explains that students will divide into partners and take turns reading paragraphs to each other from the "You Can Grow Your Intelligence" handout.

4. Students will read the first page, highlight what they think are the twelve most important words that convey the main idea, and write a one-sentence summary on the page. The teacher reminds students that good readers summarize what they read. Before having students begin, the teacher explains why it is important to only highlight a few words—it's an opportunity to develop that skill so that when they have to study in the future they won't have to read entire books, only review highlighted passages. The teacher models by highlighting one short passage as a good example of important information and one that is not, and asks students to take a minute and determine which is the better one and why. The teacher asks students to share with a partner and then some with the class.

   After students complete the first pages, the teacher will ask some students to share their summary with the entire class.

5. Next, students will take turns reading the second page aloud to their partner, again highlighting no more than twelve words, and write a summary and a question—What does the article make them wonder about? The teacher reminds students that good readers ask questions when they read. Teacher will ask some to share with the entire class.

6. Students will change partners, and then do the same thing with page three as they did with page two. In addition, they'll demonstrate the reading skill of visualizing and draw what they are seeing in their mind when they read the page. They will also describe it in words. The teacher reminds students that good readers see pictures in their mind when they read. They will also write a sentence describing their drawing. Teacher will ask some to share with the class, and bring their drawing up to the document camera.

7. With the same partner, students will read the last page, repeating the same highlighting and summarizing steps, and then demonstrate the "evaluating" reading strategy by writing whether they agree or disagree with what the article says and why (or if they like or do not like the article and why). The teacher reminds students that good readers evaluate when they read. Again, the teacher will ask some to share with the class.

8. Next, the teacher will show a short video of his/her choosing that actually shows neurons in the brain and points out that those are the things that grow when we learn something new.

9. Teacher will ask students to write a brief response to these two questions:

   ◆ Do you believe that intelligence is fixed or can grow? Why? Please use evidence from the text.

Students should use the ABC format to respond: Answer the question, Back it up with a quote, and make a Comment or Connection. (The teacher can share an ABC example on a different topic as a model. Figure 1.4 (page 18) provides a model, although the teacher might want to write her own.) It can also be called PQC: make a Point, support it with a Quote, and make a Comment or a Connection.

Students can share their responses in partners and then some can share with the class.

Assessment

A simple assessment will be to see whether or not students write a response using the ABC format. If the teacher believes a more involved assessment is necessary, he can develop a simple rubric appropriate for his classroom situation. Free online resources to both find premade rubrics and to create new ones can be found at http://larryferlazzo.edublogs.org/2010/09/18/the-best-rubric-sites-and-a-beginning-discussion-about-their-use/

Possible Extensions/Modifications

1. Students could teach what they have learned to another class. Students teaching others about this concept of being able to "grow" the brain reinforces that belief in the "teacher" (Glenn, 2010).

2. Students could make posters. The teacher could explain the difference between "literal" language ("I'm very hungry") and figurative ("I'm so hungry I could eat a horse") and ask students to take a piece of poster paper and draw a line down the middle. They could title the left side, "This Is Your Brain When It's Not Learning," and the right side, "This Is Your Brain When It Is Learning." Students could be given a choice of either drawing it literally (using images from the video used showing neurons growing and from pictures in the Brainology article) or figuratively (e.g., they could draw an unhealthy plant on the left and a blooming one on the right).

3. A few days after the lesson is completed, the teacher can ask students to write short answers to these questions and then have them share with partners: What was the most important thing you learned from the brain lesson? Was it interesting? If yes, why? If not, why not?

Ed Tech: Online Slideshow

 The teacher, after obtaining written parent permission (http://larryferlazzo. edublogs.org/2009/09/30/permission-to-use-student-work/), can scan or take photos of the posters for display on the Internet. He can make the posters into a PowerPoint and then easily upload it to a free Internet application like Slideshare (http://www.slideshare.net/).

Figure 1.4. "ABC" MODELS

Models for using the ABC framework to respond to a question (Answer the question, Back it up with a quote, then make a Comment or Connection). It can also be called PQC (make a Point, support it with a Quote, and make a Comment or a Connection).

The following two examples were responses to the question: Would you want to climb Mount Everest?

Example One

I think I would like to climb Mount Everest before I get too old. Article number 16 in the Headline Data Set, titled "The Oldest Man to Climb Mt. Everest," is about a man who is over seventy years old and is planning to be the oldest man to ever climb the mountain. It says, "Yuichiro Miura is in the midst of a three year training regimen that will include the climb to the top." I don't want to reach that age and regret not having done something I had always wanted to do. Taking risks to accomplish one's goals is what life is really all about. Plus, I don't think I want to spend three years training for anything! It won't take me as long to train now since I'm young and strong.

Example Two

If I had the time and the money, I think I would attempt to climb Everest. In the Headlines Data Set, number 8 titled "Spokane man becomes the oldest American man to climb Mt. Everest," tells about Dawes Eddy, a 66-year-old who summited Everest in 2009, becoming the oldest American man to climb the mountain. On his website it states, "When you turn 65 do you want to be over the hill or still able to climb the hill?" I think he makes a great point. Why should people stop being active or taking risks just because they are growing older? I hope I will always push myself to learn and try new things as I get older . . . because that's what life is about!

Goal-Setting Lesson Plan

Instructional Objectives

Students will:

1. Further develop their ability to practice reading strategies to help comprehend a text.

2. Understand the importance of setting goals and designing an effective action plan to achieve them.

3. Identify semester goals and an effective plan to achieve them.

Duration

One 55-minute class period and 20 minutes on the second day

Common Core English Language Arts Standards

Reading:

1. Determine central ideas or themes of a text and analyze their development; summarize the key supporting details and ideas.

2. Read and comprehend complex literary and informational texts independently and proficiently.

Writing:

1. Write arguments to support claims in an analysis of substantive topics or texts, using valid reasoning and relevant and sufficient evidence.

Speaking & Listening:

1. Prepare for and participate effectively in a range of conversations and collaborations with diverse partners, building on others' ideas and expressing their own clearly and persuasively.

Language:

1. Demonstrate command of the conventions of standard English grammar and usage when writing or speaking.

2. Demonstrate command of the conventions of standard English capitalization, punctuation, and spelling when writing

Materials

1. Copies for each student of two one-page hand-outs:

    ♦ "Harvard Business School Goal Story" (http://www. lifemastering.com/en/harvard_school.html)

    ♦ Michael Jordan Goal Story (http://www.gifted.uconn.edu/ Siegle/SelfEfficacy/Jordan.html)

2. Copies for each student of a Semester Goal Sheet, similar to the one pictured in Figure 1.1 (see page 9).

3. Copies for each student of a Weekly Goal Sheet, similar to the one pictured in Figure 1.2 (see page 10).

4. A large poster listing the key characteristics of a self-directed learner: intrinsic motivation, self-control, taking personal responsibility, metacognition/reflection, and being goal-oriented.

5. One copy of Concept Attainment examples (see Figure 1.3, page 13)

Procedure

First Day

1. Teacher writes the word "Goal" on the whiteboard. She asks students to write three things: what they think it means, a goal that they once had for themselves and that they accomplished, and what they did to accomplish it. The teacher should share an example from her life for the last two points. Students should write, and then share what they wrote with partners, and the teacher can ask a few to share with the class. The teacher then explains that the class is going to learn about goals today.

2. Teacher distributes copies of Harvard Goal Story to all students (it discusses a study that showed students who had clear goals were much more successful than those who did not make them). The teacher asks student to get into partners and take turns reading paragraphs to each other. While they are reading, they are to highlight two phrases they like in the article (not more than eight words each) and then write a one-sentence summary of the information. Then they will share both their highlighted phrases and sentence summary with another pair of students. The teacher will ask a few students share with the entire class.

3. Teacher will distribute copies of the Michael Jordan story, and students will use the same reading process.

4. Teacher will explain that students will be determining their own goals and their plans to achieve them.

5. Teacher explains that goals are divided into two categories, and that in a little while students will be making their own goals. One group can be called a "performance goal," including G.P.A., test scores, how many books you want to read, etc. The other could be described as a "learning goal," for example, wanting to be able to write better, to not be as distracted in class, etc.

6. Teacher reviews the list of characteristics of a self-directed learner on the poster that he has put on the wall. She asks students to write them down and try to define them in their own words, then share with a partner, and then discuss in class. Teacher explains that improving on these characteristics could qualify as learning goals.

Metacognition/reflection might be particularly challenging for students to understand. The teacher might want to explain it as a sort of "talking to yourself" while you're doing an activity and afterwards. You are explaining the process you are using to arrive at answers to questions, or to understand a text or concept. It's like in math class "showing your work" and not just the solution. Being aware of the process helps you spot errors you might have made, and makes you more conscious of patterns that can help you learn better. It's similar to why reading what we write out loud makes it easier to spot errors we make.

7. Teacher explains that setting goals require making a plan to achieve them, and reviews the Concept Attainment sheet using the process described in "Designing Action Plans" on page 12.

8. Teacher distributes a version of the Semester Goal Sheet and students begin to work on their form. It will be homework if not completed by the end of class.

Second Day

1. The teacher reminds students about the goals discussion from the previous day, and checks that everyone's Semester Goal Sheet is completed. The teacher then explains that students will begin to prepare a Weekly Goal Sheet focusing on one or two of the goals they listed in their Semester Goal Sheet. They will turn it in weekly to their teacher after their parents sign it. Students decide on which goal they will work on this week and what their action plan will be to achieve it.

2. The Teacher explains that each student will pick a "buddy" with whom they will review their Weekly Goal Sheet. Teacher explains that she will

review what these weekly meetings will look like the first time they do that (see Partner Support on page 11). Now, however, all the partners have to do is share what they wrote for their goals and action plans and ask their partners for any feedback/suggestions.

3. Students meet in partners, and the teacher identifies a few to share examples of what they wrote—if they are willing to make them public. The teacher writes their present grade on each sheet (perhaps using an ink stamp to sign it) and tells students they are to get their parents to sign it and return it to her by the next Friday.

Assessment

1. Students could be asked to respond to the questions: Do you think goals are important? If so, why? If not, why not? The teacher could explain they are to use the ABC (or PQC) framework to respond to the question.

2. The teacher collects each Semester Goal Sheet to make copies before returning the original to each student the following day. The teacher will assess whether or not students followed instructions for both goals and action plans and, if not, will use the concept attainment strategy again, using examples from the student goal sheets.

3. If the teacher believes a more involved assessment is necessary, she can develop a simple rubric appropriate for their classroom situation. Free online resources to both find premade rubrics and to create new ones can be found at http://larryferlazzo.edublogs.org/2010/09/18/the-best-rubric-sites-and-a-beginning-discussion-about-their-use/.

Possible Extensions/Modifications

1. Implement the idea of weekly goal sheets.

2. The teacher could ask each student to make a poster picking one of the phrases they highlighted from the two articles and illustrate it to share with other students. The posters could be placed on classroom walls as future reminders.

Ed Tech: Annotate Web Pages

Instead of printing out the articles for students to annotate, they could go to the computer lab and used a free online annotation application like Webklipper (http://webklipper.com/) or Crocodoc (http://crocodoc.com/), which allows users to write virtual sticky notes on webpages. For more information, see http://larryferlazzo.edublogs.org/2008/12/18/best-applications-for-annotating-websites/.

"Why We Should Sleep More" Lesson Plan

Instructional Objectives

Students Will:

1. Read a challenging text and demonstrate their use of reading strategies.

2. Learn the importance of getting adequate sleep.

3. Make goals for changes they want to make in their sleep patterns.

Duration

One 55-minute class period

Common Core English Language Arts Standards

Reading:

1. Determine central ideas or themes of a text and analyze their development; summarize the key supporting details and ideas.

2. Read and comprehend complex literary and informational texts independently and proficiently.

Writing:

1. Write arguments to support claims in an analysis of substantive topics or texts, using valid reasoning and relevant and sufficient evidence.

Speaking & Listening:

1. Prepare for and participate effectively in a range of conversations and collaborations with diverse partners, building on others' ideas and expressing their own clearly and persuasively.

Language:

1. Demonstrate command of the conventions of standard English grammar and usage when writing or speaking.

2. Demonstrate command of the conventions of standard English capitalization, punctuation, and spelling when writing.

Materials

1. Student copies of Sleep Survey: Part One (Figure 1.5) and Sleep Survey: Part Two (Figure 1.6, page 26).

2. Student copies of an edited and revised version of the article "Snooze or Lose" by Po Bronson (http://nymag.com/news/features/38951/). The student version should be no more than two pages. Or, if preferred, teachers can use a one-page "Read Aloud: Why Teenagers Need More Sleep" adapted from that article instead.

3. Student copies of "Read Aloud: Ways to Sleep Better" (page 26).

Procedure

1. Teacher explains that today the class is going to discuss sleep, but that going to sleep now is not part of the lesson. The teacher distributes Part One of the Sleep Survey and asks students to complete it and keep it for now.

2. Students will either:

   ♦ Divide into partners and take turns reading paragraphs to each other from the teacher-revised version of the "Snooze or Lose" article. Students will highlight no more than four words in each paragraph the show the main idea, and write a one sentence summary for each page. The teacher will ask some students to share with the entire class, or

   ♦ The teacher will show the Read Aloud adapted from the article and read it to the class and ask students to quickly write down one thing they find particularly interesting and why. Students would share with a partner, and the teacher would ask a few to share with the entire class.

3. Teacher will show and read the Read Aloud titled "Ways to Sleep Better." He will ask students to take a minute and try to think of other ways to sleep better (read before they go to sleep, etc.) and share them with a partner and then with the class.

4. Teacher will distribute Part Two of the Sleep Survey and ask students to complete it. Then, students will share what they wrote with a partner and some, if they feel comfortable sharing, can tell the class.

5. Teacher asks students to staple the two surveys together and explains that he will make copies and then return them to students to put with their semester goal sheets (if the teacher has also done that lesson).

Assessment

1. The teacher could ask students to use the ABC format to respond to the question: What is the most important thing you learned about sleep in the lesson today?

2. As an alternative, the teacher could have students create posters that could be hung around the school highlighting the negative consequences of not getting enough sleep and suggesting what students should do.

3. If the teacher feels a more involved assessment is necessary, he can develop a simple rubric for appropriate for their classroom situation. Free online resources to both find premade rubrics and to create new ones can be found at http://larryferlazzo.edublogs.org/2010/09/18/the-best-rubric-sites-and-a-beginning-discussion-about-their-use/

Possible Extensions/Modifications

1. Students could teach what they have learned to another class.

Figure 1.5. Sleep Survey: Part One

1. Your name _____

2. Your percentage grade in this class during first semester_____

3. Your overall grade-point average in all your classes during first semester _____

4. On average, how many hours of sleep do you get each night_____

5. Do you feel well-rested when you come to school in the morning? _____

6. Do you also typically feel (check one):

        Very happy _____

        Happy _____

        Okay _____

        A Little Down_____

        Very Down _____

Figure 1.6. Sleep Survey: Part Two

1. Your name _____

2. What did you learn from reading the article:

3. Do you want to increase the amount of sleep you get each night?

4. If yes, what is your goal for how much longer you want to sleep each night?

5. What are some things you can do to accomplish your goal?

Read Aloud: Why Teenagers Need More Sleep

Studies show that people younger than age twenty-one years today get an hour less of sleep each night than they did thirty years ago. Scientists have found that this loss of an hour hurts people because brains are still developing and growing until the age of twenty-one. A lot of this developing and growing happens while teenagers are asleep.

◆ Every study done shows a connection between sleep and school grades.

◆ Teenagers who get As average fifteen more minutes of sleep a night than B students.

◆ B students get eleven minutes more sleep than a night C students.

◆ C students get ten minutes more sleep than a night D students.

◆ Less sleep hurts the brain's ability to remember new information. It especially hurts the ability to learn a second language.

◆ Less sleep also tends to make you feel more depressed.

◆ Sleeping less also makes your body want to create more fat. Children who get less than eight hours of sleep are three times more likely to get fat.

Information from Bronson P. (2007, October 7). "Snooze or Lose." *New York Magazine* http://nymag.com/news/features/38951/index3.html#ixzz0 eulnLtvT

Read Aloud: Ways to Sleep Better

♦ You will sleep better if the temperature is cooler in your room.

♦ If you watch TV or use the computer in the half-hour before you go to bed, experiencing the brightness of the screen will make it more difficult for you to get to sleep.

♦ It's important to go to bed at a consistent time. If you stay up late some nights, it will make it more difficult for you to get to sleep on nights you go to bed earlier.

> Information from Merryman A. (2007, October 10). "How to get kids to sleep more." http://nymag.com/news/features/38979/

Ed Tech: Creating Online Books & Games

Students could use what they learned (or their ABC response) to create an online book for other students to read at a site like Tar Heel Reader (http://tarheelreader.org/), or an online game teaching other students about the importance of sleep using Purpose Games (http://www.purposegames.com/). For more information, visit http://larryferlazzo.edublogs.org/2009/04/01/the-best-places-where-students-can-write-for-an-authentic-audience/ and http://larryferlazzo.edublogs.org/2009/04/04/the-best-places-where-students-can-create-online-learningteaching-objects-for-an-authentic-audience/.

Helping in the Future Lesson Plan

Instructional Objectives

Students Will:

1. Use the higher-order thinking skills of categorization to identify how what they are learning in school now will help them in the future.

Duration

Twenty minutes during the first day
One 55-minute class period on the second day
Twenty minutes on the third day

Common Core English Language Arts Standards

Reading:

1. Determine central ideas or themes of a text and analyze their development; summarize the key supporting details and ideas.

Writing:

1. Write arguments to support claims in an analysis of substantive topics or texts, using valid reasoning and relevant and sufficient evidence.

Speaking & Listening:

1. Prepare for and participate effectively in a range of conversations and collaborations with diverse partners, building on others' ideas and expressing their own clearly and persuasively.

Language:

1. Demonstrate command of the conventions of standard English grammar and usage when writing or speaking.

2. Demonstrate command of the conventions of standard English capitalization, punctuation, and spelling when writing

Materials

1. The following either written on a whiteboard or displayed on an overhead projector:

   How do you think working hard and learning everything you can in this class might help you now and in the future? Please list as many possible benefits as you can. If you don't think it will benefit you, please explain why not.

2. A teacher-created data set using student responses to this question. It would look similar to Figure 1.7 (page 31). Copies for each student would be needed on the second day of this lesson.

3. Poster paper for each pair of students.

Procedure

First Day

1. Teacher displays the question and asks students to take a few minutes to write their answers.

2. Teacher asks students to share with a partner and asks some students to share with the entire class.

3. Teacher explains that the class will be doing Part Two of this lesson the next day using their responses, and collects student papers.

Second Day

1. Teacher shows a copy of the data set on the overhead and explains that students will be placing each item in the appropriate category, and highlighting a clue word that provides the reason for placing it in that category. Students will be working in partners, making columns for each category on a piece of poster paper, and then cutting-out and pasting each item under its category. Students should leave the numbers on each example as they cut them. The teacher should model using the first three examples.

2. While students are categorizing, the teacher is circulating and periodically telling a student he is going to ask her to share the numbers of the examples she has in one category—without saying the name of the category. The teacher will ask that student to share the numbers, write them on the board or overhead, and ask students to take a minute and determine what category those numbers are in. In a minute, the teacher will call on a student to say his choice and then ask the original student if he is correct.

3. After students have completed the assignment, the teacher will lead a review by asking students which category each example belongs in. There is not necessarily a single correct answer for each one if a student can make a good case for a different choice.

4. Still with their partners, students will list at least two more ways they can use what they learn in each category. The teacher will ask some students to share their answers.

5. The teacher will ask each student to pick their favorite item in each category. Then they will make a poster naming each category, listing their favorite item from each one, and illustrate it. The teacher will show a model poster. The teacher explains that students will be given a few minutes to finish it the next day, but that they should work on it that night at home.

Third Day

1. Students are given ten minutes to complete their poster and then share them. One way to do this sharing could be lining half of the students up facing the other half and each taking turns showing the other student their poster "speed-dating" style.

2. Posters are placed on classroom walls as future reminders.

Assessment

Both the categorization process and the illustrated poster have simple instructions and should be easily assessed. However, if desired, teachers can create a more detailed rubric appropriate for their classroom situation. Free online resources to both find pre-made rubrics and to create new ones can be found at http://larryferlazzo.edublogs.org/2010/09/18/the-best-rubric-sites-and-a-beginning-discussion-about-their-use/.

Possible Extensions/Modifications

1. The teacher could ask his colleagues who are teaching higher-grade levels if they would be willing to ask their students to share how they think what they learned in the earlier grade level has helped them. These responses could be shared with students who have completed this lesson plan and compared with what they listed.

2. The teacher could ask students to convert the categories into paragraphs (with topic sentences) and then into an essay.

3. To reduce the time for the entire lesson to one class period, after each student writes their responses on the first day, they could just be given the data set provided (students could be told the data set came from another class' responses). After they categorize it, they could be asked to place their ideas in the appropriate categories and then make the poster.

Ed Tech: Online Video

Students could create a short skit showing an example of how what they are learning can help them in the future. It could be videotaped with a Flip Video Recorder and posted on a class or school blog, assuming parents give their permission. See http://larryferlazzo.edublogs.org/2009/06/05/the-best-sources-for-advice-on-using-flip-video-cameras/ for information on recording skits and http://larryferlazzo.edublogs.org/2008/10/19/the-best-places-where-students-can-write-online/ for places to post them online.

Figure 1.7. Helping in the Future Data Set

Please put each of these items into one of these categories: High School, College, Career, General Life Skills. Underline a clue word that provides a reason for placing it in that category.

1. Helps me learn study skills to help in future classes.

2. Helps me learn to be a better leader.

3. Helps me read better.

4. Helps me write better.

5. It makes school work easier.

6. It makes your brain bigger.

7. It will help you get into advanced classes so it looks good on my transcript.

8. It makes my skills better.

9. Helps me get a better job.

10. Gives me better manners.

11. Have more ambition for myself.

12. Helps me speak better in front of large groups of people.

13. I'll become more self-sufficient.

14. Helps me understand more what people are writing and saying.

15. Helps me understand better the books that I read.

16. Helps me get a better job.

17. What I'm learning here can help me in a lot of other classes.

18. It will help me to do better in college English classes.

19. Helps me get a higher-paying job.

20. Working hard in this class helps me get used to working hard because I might get a job where I have to work hard all the time.

21. Helps me know how to help other people who don't understand English very well.

22. It will help me get into college.

23. Taught me how to be a hard worker.

24. It helps me outside of school to help my family.

25. The strategies I've been learning makes school work easier in the future.

26. If I have a job where I have to read and write or type, it will make it easier.

How Can You Help Students See the Importantance of Personal Responsibility?

I hear it all the time from students—it's his fault, he talked to me first; I didn't do the work because you gave bad instructions; she told me to throw the tape across the room to her. Blaming other people for their mistakes seems to come naturally to teens, and I don't know what to do about it!

This is a common lament in classrooms, and it's one of those problems that do not seem to offer many possibilities for effective immediate interventions. However, it is important for teachers to develop a response. People who tend to blame others for their own mistakes and problems will not learn from their mistakes (Bryner, 2010), are at a higher risk of being depressed, have lower achievement levels ("Q & A with Jean Twenge," n.d.), and can be perceived more negatively by others ("Viral Case of the Blame Game," 2009). Even more critically, blaming others has actually been found to be "contagious"—the more one person in a group does it, the more others around him/her will do the same (Fast & Tiedens, 2010).

> **Research shows that people who tend to blame others for their own mistakes and problems will not learn from their mistakes, are at a higher risk of being depressed, have lower achievement levels, and can be perceived more negatively by others.**

This chapter shares some potential immediate responses, along with ways to "Set The Stage." Supporting lesson plans and reproducibles are included.

Immediate Actions

Helping Students Develop a Positive Self-Image

Having a positive self-image is an important characteristic of people who take personal responsibility for their actions (Fast & Tiedens, 2010). Any of the ideas suggested in Question 1: How Do You Motivate Students? could be effective in helping students generate a greater sense of self-esteem.

Reminders

After the "Blaming Others Lesson Plan" (see page 34) is done in class, it will be easy just to say something like "Remember what we learned about blaming others," or "Remember what we learned—taking personal responsibility leads to higher achievement," or "Remember that learning from mistakes is better than blaming others" when students exhibit blaming others behavior.

Assuming you have completed the blaming others lesson, you can connect it to a reflective question (see Question 9: How Can You Best Use a Few Minutes of "Leftover" Time in Class?). Have students respond to "What do you remember from what we learned about blaming others?" or "Write about the last time you took personal responsibility and put what we learned about blaming others into action."

Writing Exercise to Build Self-Esteem

A major study on blaming others that identified its contagion danger also found that a simple writing exercise was effective in building self-esteem and increasing people's sense of personal responsibility (Fast & Tiedens, 2010).

This exercise, in which people affirmed values that were important to them, is remarkably similar to a writing exercise conducted in a different study. This study was specifically designed to assist ethnic minority students increase their self-esteem (Carey, 2009). The activity is simple, can be conducted in 15 minutes, and can be done three-to-five times during the year. It is discussed further in the "Setting The Stage" section of this chapter.

Setting the Stage

Blaming Others Lesson Plan

This lesson plan includes a series of questions connected to a quotation from President Obama, and a survey that can be used with students to help them measure their own sense of personal responsibility. Although not scientific, it can be used as a tool to get students to think about and see what personal responsibility might look like in their own lives.

Nathanael J. Fast, a University of Southern California professor, found that people could be influenced to take more personal responsibility by reading about others who have done so. In addition, he found that a simple writing activity could enhance a person's self-image, which in turn would lessen the likelihood of blaming others for their mistakes (Fast & Tiedens, 2010). These findings, along with research results cited earlier in this chapter about the effects of blaming others on the people doing the blaming, compose part of this lesson plan.

Self-Esteem Lesson Plan

As mentioned earlier in this chapter, a study found that a simple 15-minute writing activity done three-to-five times during the school year can result in long-lasting academic benefits (Cohen, Garcia, Purdue-Vaughns, Apfel, & Brzustoski, 2009). Researchers concluded that having students write about values that are important to them develops resiliency and reminds them that "their entire self-worth was not riding on a single test result" (Carey, 2009).

This lesson can be done immediately following the "Blaming Others Lesson Plan" and several other times during the year—the researchers did it at important transitional times or periods of stress such as at the beginning of semesters and before standardized testing periods (Rubenstein, 2010).

Blaming Others Lesson Plan

Instructional Objectives

Students Will:

1. Learn the negative consequences of blaming others for their mistakes and the positive effects of accepting personal responsibility.

2. Articulate these negative and positive effects in writing and verbally, and reflect on their related personal experiences and goals.

Duration

One 60-minute class period

Common Core English Language Arts Standards

Reading:

1. Determine central ideas or themes of a text and analyze their development; summarize the key supporting details and ideas.

Writing:

1. Write arguments to support claims in an analysis of substantive topics or texts, using valid reasoning and relevant and sufficient evidence.

Speaking & Listening:

1. Prepare for and participate effectively in a range of conversations and collaborations with diverse partners, building on others' ideas and expressing their own clearly and persuasively.

Language:

1. Demonstrate command of the conventions of standard English grammar and usage when writing or speaking.

2. Demonstrate command of the conventions of standard English capitalization, punctuation, and spelling when writing

Materials

1. Student copies of personal responsibility quotations sheet (Figure 2.1, page 38), Read Aloud on the effects of blaming others, the Taking Personal Responsibility questionnaire (Figure 2.2, page 39), and the Taking Personal Responsibility survey (Figure 2.3, page 41).

2. Student copies of the self-esteem writing activity (if the teacher wants to use it).

3. Document camera or overhead projector.

4. Computer project and Internet access for showing short video (optional).

Procedure

1. Teacher explains that she is going to distribute sheets sharing several quotes (Figure 2.1, page 38). In partners, she wants students to take turns reading each section to each other. Students are to write a one-sentence summary of each quote, and then write a sentence explaining whether or not they can find anything that they all have in common.

2. If desired, the teacher can play the one-minute video clip of President Obama actually saying the quote on the sheet (http://www.politico.com/news/stories/0209/18344.html).

3. After five minutes, the teacher can ask students to share their summary of one or two of the quotes, and then ask if they found anything in common. Teacher writes what students say on the board, probably something about taking responsibility for mistakes.

4. The teacher explains that, yes, those were examples of people taking responsibility for their mistakes. However, when things don't go well for us, it's easy to instead blame somebody else. Teacher gives examples from her life when she has done it. She says that in a few minutes students will get an opportunity to come up with their own similar experiences. She then explains that it can cause problems on a much bigger scale, too. Former aides to President Nixon say his tendency to blame others is what led to his disgrace, and researchers believe that placing blame and not taking personal responsibility is one of the major reasons behind major space accidents at NASA (Fast & Tiedens, 2010).

5. The teacher explains that researchers have been studying the issue of personal responsibility and blaming others. She says she would like to share what they have learned, and says she would like students to read silently with her as she reads a Read Aloud. She places the "Effects of Blaming Others" Read Aloud (page 39) on overhead or document camera and reads what it says. Afterwards, she can distribute copies to students, if desired.

6. Next, she announces that they are going to take a test to see how personally responsible they are. Students should circle one answer for each question. After they are finished, they should add their total—every time they answer number one, they get one point; for answer number two, they get two points, and for answer number three, they get three points. Tell students they should answer honestly and will not be graded on it. It is a tool to help them assess themselves.

7. The teacher distributes the questionnaire (Figure 2.2, page 39) but *not* the evaluation sheet indicating what the totals mean.

8. After a few minutes, the teacher tells students to total up their scores, and says she is now going to share what the results mean. She shows the analysis sheet on the overhead. She asks students if they agree with what the test says about their level of personal responsibility, and allows students to share their results with classmates—either in partners or with the entire class. She suggests that students keep these test results in mind when they set goals for themselves (see Question 1: How Do You Motivate Students?).

9. Next, the teacher can explain that President Obama spoke about this topic at a commencement address he gave at a high school in 2010. She can place the Taking Personal Responsibility Survey (Figure 2.3, page 41) on the overhead and reads the Obama excerpt (she also has the option of playing a video of it from the Internet; see http://www.whitehouse.gov/photos-and-video/video/president-obama-gives-commencement-address-kalamazoo-central-high-school).

10. Then the teacher can explain that students will answer the questions on the survey on their own. She reviews each question, giving her own brief answers to each one. She passes out copies of the survey.

11. After 10 minutes of students writing their answers, she asks students to get into partners and share their responses with each other. During this time, she is identifying students who have particularly thoughtful answers and telling them she will ask them to share their answers with the entire class in a few minutes.

12. After a few minutes in partners, the teacher calls on selected students to share their answers.

13. Students do the assessment activity.

Assessment

1. Students can be asked to highlight one piece of information they found most interesting using the ABC format discussed in the previous chapter (see page 17). It will be clear whether or not students have followed the format in their responses.

Possible Extensions/Modifications

1. If desired, the teacher can followup immediately with the Self-Esteem Writing Lesson Plan (see page 42).

2. Students could create a poster illustrating what they learned in the lesson.

3. The teacher could ask students to respond to this writing prompt about President Obama's comments on personal responsibility:

According to President Barack Obama, how should people react when they make mistakes in life? To what extent do you agree or disagree with his opinion? To support your essay, you can use examples from your own experiences, your observations of others, as well as any of your readings, including the president's speech.

The prompt could be accompanied with a simple graphic organizer with three boxes. The first box could say "They Say," the second could say "I Say," and the third could say "Why I Believe What I Say." That organizer is adapted from the book *They Say, I Say: The Moves That Matter In Academic Writing* by Gerald Graff and Cathy Birkenstein (W.W. Norton, 2009).

Ed Tech: Animation

 Students could create an online animation with a site like Doink (http://www.doink.com/) showing the difference between blaming someone else for a problem and accepting personal responsibility. For more information, see http://larryferlazzo.edublogs.org/2008/05/11/the-best-ways-for-students-to-create-online-animations/.

Figure 2.1. Examples of Personal Responsibility Quotations

Lippi Takes Responsibility for Failure

Italy coach Marcello Lippi took full responsibility for the reigning champions' disastrous World Cup exit following Thursday's dismal 3–2 defeat to debutants Slovakia at Ellis Park.

"I take full responsibility. There are no excuses because when a team comes to something as important as tonight's game with terror in their legs, their heads and their hearts, and they don't manage to express themselves, it means that the coach hasn't prepared them in the right way from a psychological, technical and physical perspective," he said.

"I take full responsibility, I'm sorry for everyone in Italy but obviously I haven't prepared this team well enough.

("Lippi Takes Responsibility," 2010)

Schwarzenegger Takes Responsibility for Failed Initiatives

Friday, November 11, 2005 Associated Press

SACRAMENTO—Two days after suffering a stinging election defeat, a conciliatory Gov. Arnold Schwarzenegger took responsibility for the failure of his initiatives and said he learned that he needs more patience in seeking government reform.

"The buck stops with me," he told reporters Thursday during a Capitol news conference, referring to the clean sweep against his proposals in Tuesday's special election. "I take full responsibility for this election. I take full responsibility for its failure."

("Schwarzenegger Takes Responsibility," 2005)

Read Aloud: Effects of Blaming Others

 Researchers have found that people who tend to blame others for their mistakes:

- Don't learn from their mistakes
- Are at a higher risk for being depressed
- Reach lower achievement levels
- Are liked less by their peers

In other words, by accepting personal responsibility, you:

- Learn from your mistakes
- Are less likely to become depressed
- Reach higher achievement levels
- Are liked more by your peers

Figure 2.2. Taking Personal Responsibility Questionnaire

1. Your girlfriend/boyfriend ends your relationship. Do you…

    1. Badmouth her/him to all your friends.

    2. Think he/she is a loser, but keep it to yourself.

    3. Use it as an opportunity to think about what you might have done to not be a good partner.

2. You don't do well on a test in class. Do you…

    1. Think the test is unfair and the teacher wanted students to flunk it.

    2. Not care since you're going to pass the class anyway.

    3. Think you should have studied harder.

3. You hit someone after he/she hits you, and you're sent to the office. Do you…

    1. Say the other person started it and it's not your fault.

    2. Say you don't really remember what happened.

3. Say the other person started it, but you realize you shouldn't have hit back and didn't think before you acted.

4. Who would you rather have as a friend. Someone who said…

   1. "It's the teacher's fault I got an F. He's always picking on me and is a lousy teacher."

   2. "Who cares about school? I don't need to know most of what they're teaching."

   3. "I really blew it in his class. I need to work harder."

5. Your dog bit someone after he/she tried to pet her. You…

   1. Hit and punish the dog and then get rid of her.

   2. Think the person should have asked you first before he/she tried petting her.

   3. Realize you should have trained your dog better, and decide to start right away.

6. You break a bowl in your kitchen when your mother isn't home. Do you…

   1. Blame your little brother or sister.

   2. Hope your mother doesn't discover that she's missing a bowl.

   3. Tell your mother your broke it before she finds out, say you're sorry and that you should have been more careful.

7. The teacher is giving a test. Someone talks to you and you respond. The teacher sees you talking and reduces your grade. Do you…

   1. Say the other person talked to you first, and you're tired of the teacher always picking on you.

   2. Glare at the teacher and roll your eyes, but not say anything.

   3. Say you're sorry and get back to working on the test.

8. Your homework is late because you stayed up late watching TV and playing video games instead of working on it. Do you…

   1. Think to yourself that the teacher gives too much homework, and just take a zero.

   2. Not say anything, and get the homework in the next day.

   3. Tell the teacher you blew it, and that you'd like the opportunity to make it up, but would understand if he didn't give it to you.

9. You get stopped for speeding by the police. Do you….

   1. Tell the officer that everybody else was going the same speed and why is he picking on you?

   2. Tell the officer you didn't realize what the speed limit was, and can he please, please, please give you a break.

   3. Tell the officer you're sorry, and realize you were speeding.

10. You're playing baseball or football with some friends on your street. You throw the ball and it accidentally cracks a window in a neighbor's car. Do you...

1. Run away and think to yourself they shouldn't have parked their car there, anyway.

2. Go home and tell your parents what happened and ask them what you should do.

3. Write a note saying you'll pay for the window and leave it on the car window with your name and phone number on it.

Count Up Your Score—One point for every time you answered number one, 2 points for every time you answered number two, and 3 points for every time you answered number three.

What the Score Means

If you scored between 24 and 30 points, you tend to take personal responsibility for your actions and learn from your mistakes.

If you scored between 17 and 23 points, you've got some work to do, but you have a basic understanding of what personal responsibility means.

If you scored between 10 and 16 points, you should spend more time reflecting on why personal responsibility is important and reread the information about the consequences of blaming others for your mistakes.

Figure 2.3. Taking Personal Responsibility Survey

Don't make excuses. Take responsibility not just for your successes, but for your failures as well.

The truth is, no matter how hard you work, you won't necessarily ace every class or succeed in every job. There will be times when you screw up, when you hurt the people you love, when you stray from your most deeply held values.

And when that happens, it's the easiest thing in the world to start looking around for someone to blame. Your professor was too hard; your boss was a jerk; the coach was playing favorites; your friend just didn't understand.

President Barack Obama, commencement address at Kalamazoo High School June 7, 2010

("President Obama Gives Commencement," 2010)

1. Please think about times somebody has blamed you for something, when it was really their responsibility. Write about at least one time here:

2. Please think about times when you have blamed someone else for your mistake. Write about at least one time here:

3. Please think about times when you have taken responsibility for your mistakes. Write about at least one time here:

4. Next time you feel like blaming someone, what could you do instead? What could help you remember to do this?

5. If I take more personal responsibility, and blame others less, I think it will make me feel _____.

Self-Esteem Writing Lesson Plan

Instructional Objectives

Students Will:

Practice their writing skills and develop their self-esteem by writing about a value important to them.

Duration

Fifteen minutes, five times during the school year

Common Core English Language Arts Standards

Writing:

1. Write routinely over extended time frames (time for research, reflection, and revision) and shorter time frames (a single sitting or a day or two) for a range of tasks, purposes, and audiences.

Speaking & Listening:

1. Prepare for and participate effectively in a range of conversations and collaborations with diverse partners, building on others' ideas and expressing their own clearly and persuasively.

Language:

1. Demonstrate command of the conventions of standard English grammar and usage when writing or speaking.

2. Demonstrate command of the conventions of standard English capitalization, punctuation, and spelling when writing

Materials

1. Student copies of handouts shown in Figure 2.4 (page 45).

2. Document camera or overhead projector to display all of the figures.

Procedure

1. Teacher asks students to think for a minute and write down what they think a "value" is (explain she is not talking in mathematical terms).

2. Teacher asks students to quickly tell a student near them what they wrote.

3. Teacher asks for definitions and helps clarify that it is something that is important, valuable and desirable. Generally, it is something you believe in. She explains that it is easy to get distracted by everyday life and forget about what is really important to us, so that several times during the year the class is going to do a little thinking and writing about their values.

4. She shows students the first page of Figure 2.4 (page 45), the list of values, reads them aloud, and says she is going to give each of them a copy and they should circle one that is most important to them. Teacher distributes the sheets.

5. Next, the teacher puts the "Thinking of a Time" portion on the other overhead and explains that students are to think about times in their lives when the value they circled was important to them, and to write a few sentences about what happened and why it was important to them. The teacher can tell students that they can change the value they circled if they want. The teacher distributes the "Thinking of a Time" portion.

6. After a few minutes, the teacher shows the "Agree or Disagree" section of Figure 2.4 (page 45) on the overhead and tells students she is going to give them their own copies and they should write down their response to each statement. Teacher gives the third sheet to students.

7. Teacher asks students to share their responses with a partner, and asks selected students to share with the class if they feel comfortable doing so.

8. Students staple their sheets in order and teacher collects them.

Assessment

1. Because this activity is focused on building student self-esteem and should only take a few minutes, the key assessment is whether or not students completed the sheets and took the questions seriously. No other assessment tool is needed.

Possible Extensions/Modifications

1. It is recommended that a similar lesson be done five times during the year. Changes done by the original researchers included having students write about two or three important values, giving different lists of values, or asking students to write about which values might be most important during a certain time period, like Winter Break (Cohen et al., 2009).

2. Students can create a poster illustrating their most important value or values.

Ed Tech: Comic Strip

 Students can create an online comic strip illustrating their key value and an occasion when it was important to them. There are many free and simple applications available. Go to http://larryferlazzo.edublogs.org/2008/06/04/the-best-ways-to-make-comic-strips-online/ to learn more.

Figure 2.4. Handouts

Values

Your Name _____

Date _____

Circle the ONE value that is most important to you:

athletic ability

being good at art

being smart or getting good grades

creativity

independence

living in the moment

membership in a social group (such as your community, racial group, or school club)

music

politics

relationships with friends or family

religious values

sense of humor

Thinking of a Time

Please think about a specific time when the value you circled was important to you. When was that time, and why was it important to you then? Please write a few sentences.

Agree or Disagree

How strongly do you agree or disagree with each of the three statements at the bottom of the page. Pick one of these words/phrases and write it next to each of the statements.

Very Strongly Agree

Strongly Agree

Agree

Strongly Disagree

Very Strongly Disagree

- ♦ "This value has influenced my life"
- ♦ "In general, I try to live up to this value"
- ♦ "This value is an important part of who I am"

How Do You Deal With a Student Who Is Being Disruptive in Class?

John is having a bad day. He isn't paying attention to what you're saying; he's making noises, throwing pieces of paper when he doesn't think you're looking, and is trying to distract other students. And he certainly isn't focusing on doing his own work. When you divide the class into pairs, he talks to students around him about other topics instead of talking with his partner about the assignment. He's cracking jokes that are making other students laugh and getting them off-task. You've asked him to pay attention numerous times, but nothing seems to work.

There are multiple ways to respond to this challenging situation. A typical, and understandable, reaction to this kind of behavior is threatening John with punishment (detention, a referral to the office, phoning home) and then following through with the threat. There are obvious serious student transgressions that may call for this kind of punishment consequence (a physical altercation, sexual harassment, threat of physical violence, if the student is completely out of control). However, there are numerous occasions where punishment may only work temporarily, may not work at all, or may only exacerbate the problem, and not solve it.

> **More often than not, punishment may teach that it is just important to not be caught next time and result in more student distraction and disengagement from work and a lesser feeling of personal responsibility (Lewis, Romi, Qui, & Katz, 2005).**

Marvin Marshall, author of *Discipline Without Stress, Punishment or Rewards* (2001), provides this guidance for teachers: "Will what I am about to do or say bring me closer or will it push me away farther from the person with whom I am communicating?" (Marshall, n.d.)

Keeping that advice in mind, what follows are alternative ways to respond to a disruptive student. Bear in the mind that one might work like magic for John, but not at all for Sally. Or, they may work for a student on one day but not the next. These are suggestions for teachers to keep in their "toolbox"—the more tools, the better. As the saying goes, "If the only tool we have is a hammer, then every problem looks like a nail." In some ways, an effective teacher needs to have an individual strategic plan for each student.

The suggestions are divided into three sections. The first shares ways to respond to an immediate situation and quickly (one hopes) get the student reengaged in the learning process. It is important to have a conversation with the student and help the student think through ways that he (and, in many instances, the teacher) can handle specific challenging situations better. However, it is often better to have those conversations later in class, later that day, or twenty-four hours later after everyone has calmed down.

The second section shares ways to "set the stage" early to help preempt disruptions before they occur. The third section discusses what to do if none of the ideas in the first two sections are working.

In addition, two reproducibles are included, as well as a lesson plan.

Immediate Actions

Reflection Cards

Some teachers give a sheet to students to write about what happened, why it happened, and what the student could have done differently. It may work for some, but many students are not going to be thinking clearly at that moment, and much of the time they don't really know why they did it, anyway. That is not to say a writing exercise can't be helpful. It can, just with a different focus.

Numerous studies have found that self-control is a resource that can often be used more quickly than the brain can replenish it. Researchers found that people who were put in a situation where they had to demonstrate self-control for a longer time would more easily give up trying to complete a complex task they were given afterwards. The researchers concluded that self-control is a "limited energy resource" that can get depleted (Gailliot, 2007). These studies found several ways to provide that needed resupply.

One came to this conclusion: "The recipe is simple. If you are feeling happy, focus on reasons why those feelings will last, and if you are feeling unhappy, focus on reasons why those feelings will pass" (How to stop overindulging, 2009). Another found that self-affirmation refueled the self-control of study participants. The participants wrote about their core values—whatever was important to them (family, friends, etc.) ("Self-Control Instantly Replenished," 2010).

One way to use these research results in the classroom is through "Reflection Cards" (Figure 3.1).

Figure 3.1. Reflection Card

REFLECTION CARD

NAME _____ DATE _____

1. Please write at least three sentences about a time (or times) you have felt successful and happy:

2. Please write at least three sentences about something that is important to you (friends, family, sports, etc.) and why it's important:

When students are being disruptive, teachers can ask them to take the cards (printed on card stock) outside and briefly write answers to questions about moments when they were happy and what values they believe are important. Students are removed from the immediate situation and distracted in a positive way. After they have completed it, they can return to the classroom, return the card to the teacher, and, with luck, their self-control capacity will be replenished.

In a future conversation with the student, the teacher can encourage him/her to try to recognize on their own when they are "low" on self-control and to think of responses to those questions without requiring teacher intervention. With this strategy, and with others in this chapter, it would be important to share with students the reasons and research behind the ideas—at a time when everyone is calm.

Emphasizing "Positive-Framed" Messages

Recent research ("The Influence of Positive," 2010) shows that that "loss-framed messages" (if you do this, then something bad will happen to you) really don't have the "persuasive advantage" that they are thought to have. Positive-framed messages (if you do this, all this good stuff will happen to you) are more effective. Researchers suggest the reason is because people "don't like to be bullied into changing...behavior." This is similar to the reason why incentives tend not to increase behavior that requires higher-order thinking—people don't want to feel like mice in a maze.

It certainly reflects my experience with classroom management. I have had much better success talking with students about how changing their behavior will help them achieve their goals (passing a class, graduating from high school, going to college, etc.) than with threatening negative consequences (although, admittedly, in some circumstances, that might work and I have used it). If you have already taught the marshmallow lesson on self-control (see "Self-Control Lesson Plan," page 57), a more gentle loss-framed message might be "Connie, remember how successful the people were who didn't eat the marshmallow?". Using the regular goal-setting strategies listed in Question 1: How Do You Motivate Students? can be a good tool in developing these kinds of "positive-framed messages." Assuming you have already taught the goal-setting lesson in that chapter, you can remind the students (very quietly and in a respectful tone) of their self-determined goals and ask them if they think their behavior is going to help accomplish them. It is focusing on what *they* have identified as their self-interest—not on a goal anyone else has set for them. Some teachers might even want to consider placing a poster on their wall saying, "Is What I'm Doing, or What I'm Thinking of Doing, Going to Help Me Accomplish My Goals?" If the poster is there, asking the student to look at it might be an adequate intervention. Studies show that thinking about possible future events strengthens one's self-control capacity (Lehrer, 2010). Interestingly enough, self-control appears to be strengthened more by focusing on the goal itself, rather than by thinking about how to achieve it ("How to Improve," 2008).

Emphasizing What Students *Can* Do Instead of What They *Can't* Do

Avoidant instruction is the term used to describe the action of emphasizing what people cannot do—"Don't walk on the grass" and "Don't chew gum." Some researchers recommend that a more effective way to get the desired behavior is to instead emphasize what you want people to do, rather than what you do not want them to do (Russell & Grealy, 2010).

For example, if a student asks to go the restroom, but the timing is not right for the lesson, the teacher could respond, "Yes, you can. I just need to have you wait for a few minutes," instead of just saying, "No." Or, if a student is talking at an inappropriate time, instead of just telling the student to "Be quiet!" or "Stop talking!" the teacher could go over and quietly say, "I'm glad you have a lot of energy today. You'll be able to talk and use that energy in a few minutes when we break into small groups. Now, though, I'd appreciate your listening."

This kind of positive, less-confrontational response might be less likely to cause an already disruptive student to escalate a problem.

Telling Students That You Are *Not* Going to Call Their Parents

Instead of calling parents of a student who is not behaving well, consider privately telling a student who is behaving inappropriately that you will *not* call home that day. Instead, tell them that you are going to call their home in a week, that you want to just say good things about them, and they have a week to show they could be the kind of student you know they could be. Before the call, tell the students specifically what you will be recognizing (see Question 5: How Do You Help Students See Problems as Opportunities, Not Frustrations?)

Physical Proximity, Saying "Please," Compliance Recognition, & Requests Instead of Orders

Much classroom management research has shown three common elements in efforts to have students stop disruptive behavior. One is the teacher having close physical proximity to the student being approached, another is including the word "please" in the student's direction, and a third is positive recognition when the student complies (Rathvon, 2008). Again, these are also positive behavior models for all students.

Saying "Thank you" (while being explicit about the action you are thanking the student for doing—see Question 5: How Do You Help Students See Problems as Opportunities, Not Frustrations?) can provide immediate positive reinforcement to the student. People who are thanked by authority figures are more likely to be cooperative, to feel more valued, and to have a greater sense of self-confidence because of that kind of recognition (Sutton, 2008). In addition, the act of saying "thank you" generates positive feelings in the speaker for the person they are thanking (Herbert, 2010). Enhancing the positive view a teacher has for their students can never be a bad thing.

Although some researchers differ, more recent studies (Yong, 2010) and the author's personal experience indicate that students—and most people— are more likely to comply with a task (and do so more quickly) if *asked* to do so instead of being *told*. Saying to Bob, "Can you please sit down?" in a calm voice may be more effective than "Sit down." Community organizers have a saying: "If you don't give people the opportunity to say no, you don't give them the opportunity to say yes, either." By framing it as a request, the teacher can help reinforce what William Glasser calls the student's need for autonomy (Van Tassell, 2004) and help them "own" the action. This sense of ownership may increase the student's commitment to staying on task, and again serves as a behavior model.

Remaining Calm

It is easy for a teacher to become frustrated and react out of anger—we are only human. However, that response can often result in actions that do not lead to the desired results. By taking three deep breaths and trying to think of something relaxing before responding, a teacher increases his/her likelihood of taking a more effective action, along with modeling appropriate behavior for all his/her students to see (Joseph & Strain, 2006).

No matter what option a teacher chooses to use, he/she will have more success by speaking softly and respectfully to the student—ideally going over to the student so that only the student can hear what is being said. Yelling has been found to cause "downshifting" in the brain of the target of the anger. This shuts down higher cognitive functions, resulting in limited, if any, learning, and the "fight or flight" response ("Yelling at Students Does Not Improve," 2010).

Setting the Stage

Replenishing Glucose

Researchers have connected loss of self-control to a loss of glucose—the subject's brain used glucose more quickly than it could be replenished when it was exerting self-control for that period of time. They conclude that eating food that releases glucose over an extended period of time, such as complex carbohydrates, could serve as an effective way to gain more glucose and self-control (Gailliot, 2007). Providing certain students facing self-control challenges with a handful of trail mix or a graham cracker with peanut better before class or between periods could be one way to put this research into practice. Then, if it appears to be working, encouraging students to make a point of eating breakfast or bringing their own snacks could be a next step.

Asking Students How They Feel During Good Moments

After a student has had a good day demonstrating self-control, a teacher can ask how they feel at that time. Generally, a student will say something positive in response. A teacher can then ask the student to remember that feeling, and ask them to contrast it with how they feel after a bad day.

Helping students become aware of the more positive feelings they experience when they're doing well might be more effective than asking them why they're doing what they're doing when they are having a bad day.

Teachers calling a student's home after the student has done well can be very helpful with this tactic. A teacher can ask the student how they felt about the call and how they thought the call made the parents feel. Again, the student will usually say something positive. The teacher telling them, "I want to make more of those kinds of calls home" can be another variation on this idea.

Stress Balls

Using a stress ball has been found to reduce disruptive behavior (Stalvey & Brasell, 2006) and providing a small one that fits into a student's pocket is an option to consider. Of course, some students might not be able to resist the temptation to throw them, so the stress ball has to be used selectively and with clear rules for its usage. Students also need to be shown that they need to squeeze and release repeatedly, and not just squeeze until the ball breaks.

Writing Students a Letter

I periodically write personal letters to students—especially to students who are facing particular challenges. I place the letter in a sealed envelope with the student's name on it, and just give it to the student in a matter-of-fact way. I've been amazed at the effect these letters have had. Here are two samples:

Letter One

Dear _____,

You are a young man with many gifts:

♦ When you decide you want to do something, you can push away any distractions and get it done, and get it done well.

♦ When you want to smile, it lights up the entire room and makes everyone who sees you feel better.

♦ When you want to help someone, you have a talent for helping them learn how to do it for themselves and not just do it for them.

♦ When things might not be going great, and you are willing to open up and show how you are really feeling about something, it makes people around you want to do everything they can to help you and connect with you.

When you do these things, you become every teacher's delight and a delight to all your classmates. When you do these things, I want to go the extra mile, and more, to help you achieve everything and anything you want to.

I hope you will want to do these things, and show your gifts, more and more.

Mr. Ferlazzo

Letter Two

Dear _____,

You clearly have what's called the "work ethic"—the commitment to work hard—and the intelligence to be a star in school and in life.

I also appreciate your cheerfulness and your respectful attitude. I really enjoy having you in class.

Other students see you as a leader. That is a gift and a responsibility. You are a role model.

By having all the qualities I mentioned, you are a great role model.

By having a just a little more self-control, you can be a star role model.

I hope you decide to be a star.

Mr. Ferlazzo

Have Students "Pack Away Their Troubles"

Some studies show that if you put something in an envelope or box that relates to a previous disappointment, it helps people get past those negative feelings ("Packing Your Troubles Away," 2010). One researcher said: "If you tell people, 'You've got to move on,' that doesn't work. What works is when people enclose materials that are relevant to the negative memories they have. It works because people aren't trying to explicitly control their emotions" (para. 3).

Teachers could ask a student to take a few minutes and write and/or draw about the problems they've been having in class—not doing homework, not focusing, disruptive behavior, etc.—and then have the student put what they've written in an envelope as a symbolic move to "get rid of it" and get a new start. Of course, depending on when during the grading period this activity is done, it might even be more effective if it is combined with a grade increase to an A to emphasize the "new" start.

Self-Control Lesson Plan

The self-control lesson plan in this chapter uses the famous "Don't Eat the Marshmallow" experiment by Dr. Walter Mischel (and replicated by others). This lesson demonstrates how developing self-control is in the self-interest of students, and is done in an engaging and humorous way.

What if None of These Strategies and Tactics Work?

Of course, few—if any—of these tactics will work if a teacher has not developed a trusting relationship with his/her students. Numerous researchers, including Robert Marzano (2007, p. 150), have documented that in many ways the quality and quantity of trust in the classroom is the key to everything that happens inside its walls.

Teachers can begin to build these kinds of relationships in numerous ways, such as:

- Making a point of having an individual one-minute "check-in" with two or three students each day to learn what is going on in their lives.

- Having students complete a student survey (see Figure 3.2 for an example) at the beginning of the school year (and another one in midyear as interests and goals change), and using the information in the surveys to initiate specific conversations, make book recommendations, or craft interventions (perhaps with the assistance of a school counselor and/or a parent).

- Speaking with a teacher who has one of your students at a different time of the day when you might have a free period, and arranging to take the student out of that class for a few minutes to take a short walk and chat about how the student is doing.

- Making a home visit to the student and the student's family (see Ferlazzo & Hammond, 2009). Another benefit to having contact with the parent is that the teacher can learn from the parents' years of experience about what strategies—both in and out of school—have worked well with their child.

There may very well be instances where a teacher has tried all the ideas listed in the chapter (and more!), but a student continues to be disruptive (at a lower level than previously, but still disruptive). At that point, for the good of that student, the rest of the class, and for the teacher's own sanity, it might be time to move toward the use of operant conditioning (Mahto, 2006)—in other words, carrots and sticks. "Sticks" are fairly obvious to most of us, so the bulk of this section emphasizes identifying and using "carrots."

Question 1: How Do You Motivate Students? and Question 4: How Do You Regain Control of an Out-of-Control Class? discuss the ramifications of this type of behavior management—that it can work effectively to control basic "mechanical" actions like simple behavior, but can stifle the development of higher-order thinking skills. For that reason, it is important for the

Figure 3.2. Student Survey

Name _____

Class _____

INTRODUCING YOURSELF

Please take some time to thoughtfully answer these questions. Your answers will help me begin to get to know you. If you run out of space, please feel free to write on the back. Thank you.

YOUR FULL NAME _____

WHAT YOU WOULD LIKE TO BE CALLED _____

YOUR ADDRESS & HOME PHONE NUMBER:

_____

_____

_____

YOUR PARENTS' WORK PHONE NUMBERS: _____

YOUR BIRTHDAY _____

1. What do you most look forward to when you wake up in the morning and why?

2. What do you like to do in your free time and why?

3. When you think about life after you graduate from school (high school or college) what career sounds good to you and why?

4. What things do you feel like you do well—in school and away from school?

5. What is your favorite poem, short story, novel, or essay, and why do you like it?

6. What are the *three* most important goals you would like to accomplish by next June (10 months from now)? These could be related to school or related to other parts of your life. Why are they important to you?

teacher to have a plan to eventually "wean" the student off the system before initiating this kind of effort.

One way to begin is to have a conversation with the student and first ask him/her what they think about their behavior and work in class. You can then explain that you want him/her to be successful, but that you're concerned that things are going in the wrong direction. You could ask what they think they need to succeed—in other words, find out what would make it "worth their while" to behave. I have made contracts with different students to exempt them temporarily from homework, to let them leave a minute or two early for lunch, to pay them to come to school early one day each work to do work for me so they can save money to buy a skateboard, etc. When these students have begun to revert to their previous behavior, I then just had to say "Remember our agreement," which is a lot more energizing to the student (and to me) than directly challenging the student on a specific behavior.

In the course of developing and implementing that kind of arrangement, the teacher and student can talk about the fact that these are temporary arrangements that are designed to move them toward developing the self-control they will need to achieve the goals that they have said they want to achieve.

There are numerous other "carrots" and ways to use them. For example, if the student is indeed concerned about his/her grade, each day the student could be given a sticky note to place on his/her desk. For every 15 minutes they are not doing the targeted behavior and are acting appropriately, and you do not have to say anything to him/her to get them on track, they put a mark on the sticky note. At the end of each day, they give the sticky note to you and receive a certain number of extra credit points for each mark.

It is also important to focus on changing just one behavior at a time. By being successful in one change first, that accomplishment will increase the chance of additional successful changes. This kind of strategy is needed because the part of our brain responsible for willpower just has too many other responsibilities—it can only handle so much more:

> The brain area largely responsible for willpower, the prefrontal cortex, is located just behind the forehead. While this bit of tissue has greatly expanded during human evolution, it probably hasn't expanded enough. That's because the prefrontal cortex has many other things to worry about....For instance, scientists have discovered that this chunk of cortex is also in charge of keeping us focused, handling short-term memory and solving abstract problems. (Lehrer, 2009, December 26)

Studies also show that people are who are angry are more attentive to rewards than to threats ("People Who Are Angry Pay More Attention," 2010).

"Rewards" can include all the ideas listed in this chapter, including reminding students that by focusing they can meet their goals, that the teacher knows they are not acting like the kind of person they really are, and that the teacher wants to be able to give them an A in class.

> **"Sticks" are easy. If teachers have to resort to this method, perhaps we could spend a little more time being creative with the "carrots."**

Self-Control Lesson Plan

Instructional Objectives

Students Will:

1. Read a challenging text and demonstrate their use of reading strategies.

2. Gain an understanding of the advantages of mastering self-control and strategies for maintaining it.

3. Make a short presentation explaining what they have learned and how they will use that knowledge in their own lives.

Duration

One 55-minute class period
Thirty minutes on the following day (optional)

Common Core English Language Arts Standards

Reading:

1. Determine central ideas or themes of a text and analyze their development; summarize the key supporting details and ideas.

Writing:

1. Write arguments to support claims in an analysis of substantive topics or texts, using valid reasoning and relevant and sufficient evidence.

Speaking & Listening:

1. Prepare for and participate effectively in a range of conversations and collaborations with diverse partners, building on others' ideas and expressing their own clearly and persuasively.

Language:

1. Demonstrate command of the conventions of standard English grammar and usage when writing or speaking.

2. Demonstrate command of the conventions of standard English capitalization, punctuation, and spelling when writing.

Materials

♦ Enough copies for each student of the first two-and-one-half pages of *Don't! The Secret of Self-Control* by Jonah Lehrer (http://www.newyorker.com/reporting/2009/05/18/090518fa_fact_lehrer?printable=true)

♦ Computer projector and computer access to show the six-minute video "Joachim de Posada says, Don't eat the marshmallow yet" (http://www.ted.com/talks/joachim_de_posada_says_don_t_eat_the_marshmallow_yet.html)

♦ Enough copies of a shorter excerpt from the Lehrer article (the last section discussing strategies to distract oneself from temptation) (http://larryferlazzo.edublogs.org/2009/10/22/i-like-this-lesson-because-it-make-me-have-a-longer-temper-part-one/)

♦ Poster paper and color markers or pencils

♦ Two pieces of candy for each student

Procedure

First Day

1. Teacher writes "Self-Control" on board and asks students to take a minute and write down what they think it means. Students then share their responses with a neighbor. Teacher walks around room identifying students to call on to share what they wrote.

2. Teacher then "play acts" wanting to throw a pencil at somebody but restrains himself. Teacher also gives examples of when he demonstrated self-control in his life, and times when he did not.

3. Teacher asks students to write about at least one time when they did not exhibit self-control and share with a partner and with the class.

4. Teacher asks students to write about times when they did show self-control and share.

5. Teacher gives instructions prior to distributing the first two-and-a-half pages of *The New Yorker* article. Students will read in pairs, taking turns reading paragraphs aloud to each other. After finishing each paragraph, students will underline or highlight no more than six words that demonstrate the main idea. Students will then write one summary sentence for each page. Prior to having students begin work, the teacher will highlight two phrases—one a good example and one a bad example—in the first paragraph and ask students to pick the good example and explain why it is good. The teacher will also explain to the students the importance of highlighting key words—it is a skill that will help them in other classes so that when they have to study the will not have to reread the entire text. The teacher stops students twice to have some share their summary sentences.

6. Teacher puts a piece of candy on each student's desk, and tells them if it's still there at the end of class they will get a second piece.

7. Teacher once again "play acts" wanting to throw a pencil at someone. This time, however, he articulates strategies he would use to strengthen his self-control (I want teachers to say I'm a good student; I want to get an A in this class; I don't want to do that because I remember when that student was nice to me; It would make me sad if he was hurt).

8. Teacher shows the six-minute video from *TED Talks* of a similar experiment.

9. Teacher gives the second short excerpt from *The New Yorker* article (which talks about strategies to avoid "eating the marshmallow). Students are told to read it in pairs and highlight no more than six words in each paragraph. They are also told to summarize the main points in two or three sentences, and share what they wrote with another pair of students.

Second Day

1. Teacher asks students to take a minute and remember what they learned the previous day about self-control. The teacher explains that he is going to assign partners, and he wants each partner to explain to the other what they learned. Each partner, though, will function as a teacher, and grade how well the other one did (the teacher can clarify that the grade will not be recorded, and treat it in a light-hearted manner). After partners share with each other, the teacher can ask which students received an A, which a B, etc., and then ask for students to share what they remembered.

2. The teacher then shows a model poster he made of himself being a student. One half is titled "When I Want To Do This" and the other side is titled "Instead, I'll Do This." For example, the first side can show a pic-

ture of himself throwing a pencil in class with the sentence "When I Want To Throw A Pencil In Class…." The other side can show him thinking "I want to do well in this class" with a headline saying "Instead, I'll Think Of How Much I Like Being In This Class." Students are told to think of a time when they did not show self-control—they can use the example they had already written about or think of another one. The teacher can ask them to think about when they want to do something bad—either in school, at home, with friends, etc. They are to draw it on one half of the paper. On the other half of the paper, they are to draw what they can do instead and include a "thought bubble" showing how they could divert themselves from losing control.

3. Students work on their poster then share them. One way to do this sharing would be to line up the students in two facing rows and have students take turns showing the their poster "speed-dating" style.

4. Posters are placed on classroom walls as future reminders.

   NOTE: Instead of using class time to make the posters, students could be given the assignment as homework.

Assessment

1. It should be simple to determine whether or not students followed instructions in the partnered reading and for the posters. If the teacher believes a more involved assessment is necessary, he can develop a simple rubric for appropriate for their classroom situation. Free online resources to both find premade rubrics and to create new ones can be found at http://larryferlazzo.edublogs.org/2010/09/18/the-best-rubric-sites-and-a-beginning-discussion-about-their-use/.

2. Students could be asked to highlight one piece of information they found most interesting using the ABC or PQC format discussed in Question 1: How Do You Motivate Students? It will be clear if students have followed the format or not in their responses.

Possible Extensions/Modifications

1. Periodically during the year, the teacher can ask students to reflect in writing and verbally on the most recent times they have "not eaten the marshmallow" and what strategies they used to exhibit self-control.

2. A few days after the lesson is completed, the teacher can ask students to write short answers to the following questions and then have them share with partners: What was the most important thing you learned from the marshmallow lesson? Was it interesting? If yes, why? If no, why not?

3. Students could watch another short video titled "Mind In The Making" (http://www.youtube.com/watch?v=Lu1V9GM6BXE). There are two things that make this video stand out. One, it shows Dr. Walter Mischel, the originator of the experiment, actually saying what the long-term implications of the test might be. Because students read about him in the lesson, it could have a double impact. Second, the video shows a fun "reverse Simon Sez" activity designed to help children develop self-control skills. It is obviously designed for small children, but even high school students might enjoy doing it for a few minutes after they see the video.

4. If the teacher wants to reinforce the value of self-control with a future short lesson, he could use a Read Aloud from a recent study on grades and self-control (Tangney, Baumeister, & Boone, 2004). The teacher could show on the overhead an excerpt that showed similar results to the marshmallow study: "Higher scores on self-control correlated with a higher grade point average, higher self-esteem,…less binge eating and alcohol abuse, better relationships and interpersonal skills." The teacher could ask students to respond to the question: "Why do you think people with more self-control would gain these kinds of benefits?"

5. Small groups of students could create two one-minute "skits" of their posters—one showing them giving in to the "bad" temptation, and the other showing what they would do to resist it.

Ed Tech: 3D Movies

 Students could easily create an online 3D movie showing the two alternatives they highlighted in their poster by using the free http://www.xtranormal.com/ Web 2.0 application using its text-to-speech feature. For more information, go to http://larryferlazzo.edublogs.org/2008/10/23/the-best-new-sites-students-should-use-with-supervision/.

Question 4

How Do You Regain Control of an Out-of-Control Class?

I dread coming to school. I've worked hard at getting to know the students I teach, but the class won't listen to me much of the time. Students throw paper and pencils at each other, and many don't do their work. When I get angry and yell it just seems to make things worse. I just don't know what to do!

I have "been there and done that," and it may have been the worst time in my teaching career. None of the tools in my "toolbox" of classroom management strategies were working, and I didn't know what to do.

So I asked for help, and received it from Jim Peterson, a very talented administrator at our school. He also happens to be a behavioral therapist and a clinical hypnotherapist. Jim suggested a classroom management system, which he had been developing, that is the best I have seen in regaining control of an out-of-control class. The way it is described in this chapter contains some modifications to his system, primarily with additional positive reinforcement opportunities and "weaning" students off of it, but the vast majority is his design.

It uses a "carrots-and-sticks" approach, and the long-term negative consequences of this method are made clear in Question 1: How Do You Motivate Students? However, in extreme circumstances (see Question 3: How Do You Deal With a Student Who Is Being Disruptive in Class?) a *temporary* use of rewards and punishments may be one of the few practical options available. Although it may be a challenge, it can be a path that leads toward developing more intrinsic motivation. This path is critical because, as discussed in the motivation chapter, although carrots and sticks can be effective in motivating mechanical behavior (such as complying with instructions), it will not enhance higher-thinking skills.

How It Works

The main idea behind Jim's system is using points to immediately reinforce positive behavior and to immediately punish negative behavior, but doing it in a way that is not disruptive to the flow of the class. Rapid feedback has a major effect on student work and behavior—whether or not it's in a carrots-and-sticks environment (DiSalvo, 2010, March 11)—so timeliness is a critical factor in the method's success.

In Jim's system, class time is divided into sections and students can earn up to fifty points per section. For example, a sixty-minute class period can be divided into two thirty-minute sections for a total of 100 points. Or, perhaps the class typically does three major activities during that time and it is divided into three sections for a total of 150 points each day.

Students begin with 50 points for each section and maintain that point total if they are on task, following instructions, and not being disruptive. They are constantly "paid" verbally (you could also call it a "vocal stamp") —"John, I'd like you to keep your fifty points so far," etc.—and on a clipboard. If students are not following instructions, the teacher says, "John, I'd like you to keep your forty-five points so far." (Thirty points is probably the lowest you want to go. At that point a different intervention, such as removing the student from class, might be appropriate.) This kind of verbal "payout" (and reduction) occurs constantly during class. Once points are lost during a section, students can "earn them back" by becoming refocused in their subsequent behavior (I always hope that all students can get their full fifty points). At the end of each class period students are told their point total (a modification to Jim's system that I made).

Keeping track of the numbers is made easier by using a weekly form that Jim developed (see Figure 4.1, page 64) that is on the teacher's clipboard.

Figure 4.1. Classroom Diagram

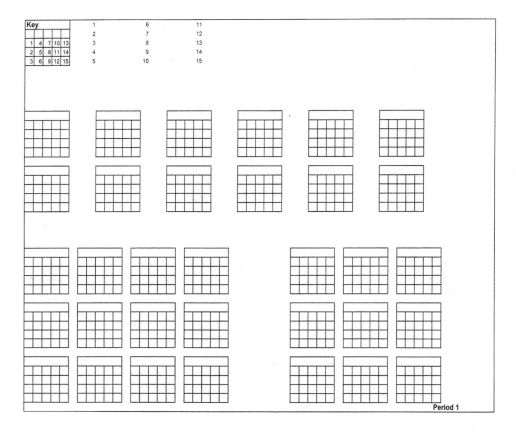

Published with permission of Jim Peterson.

You can design the sheet in whatever way you have a classroom setup. Figure 4.2 is an enlarged part of that form that is one student's portion.

The name of the student goes in the long rectangular box at the top. Each of the five vertical columns is for one day of the week. The four boxes in each column are for each section of class that is worth fifty points (as mentioned earlier, a teacher can reduce those to two or three sections).

The teacher can use whatever tracking system he/she is most comfortable with. One strategy is not leaving any mark when students have their full fifty points, and just make small lines in the boxes when one loses five points (and then erase them if and when they earn it back again). It does not really require much record keeping, as the goal is to keep the paper as blank as possible.

Figure 4.2. A Student Portion

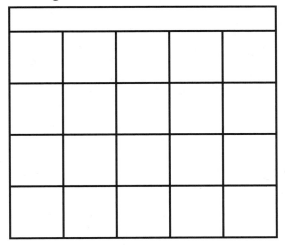

Published with permission of Jim Peterson.

A key component of ensuring the success of this system is making expectations very clear prior to the beginning each graded "section." For example, if students are going to work in partners for thirty minutes on reading an article and answering questions or doing a project on it, the teacher might say "I want everyone to get their fifty points for this next section. Here is what you will have to do to get them," and then list these directions and expectations on the whiteboard or overhead:

1. Be facing your partner and starting to take turns reading each paragraph in the article within ninety seconds after I say "begin."

2. Demonstrating a reading strategy of your choice—visualizing, making a connection, evaluating, summarizing, asking a question—in writing next to each paragraph.

3. Only talking with your partner.

4. Staying in your seat.

Note that the directions relate to both the academic task and the behavioral expectations.

While the students are working, the teacher circulates, constantly saying "John, you have your fifty points so far," "Sally, you have your forty-five points so far," etc. It is seldom necessary to say why the point total has been reduced because the directions are clear and generally students know whether or not they are following them. If there is a protest, the teacher just has to say, "I want you to earn your points back. You can do that just by looking at the directions and following them."

Behavior can begin changing quite quickly. Many students who previously gained their gratification through talking and disrupting the class, now can get it through gaining points.

Beginning the System

If possible, it is probably best to begin this new system in the context of a "fresh start." For example, students can enter the class with a new seating arrangement on the board the day the system begins. The teacher might even announce that with this fresh start, everyone's grade is going back to an A. These actions communicate to students that things are going to change, and they put many into a positive frame of mind. The teacher can explain that he hasn't felt good about how the class has been going, and he wants to try something new that he thinks students will like. He can also say that it should make it easier for students to maintain good grades, too.

After quickly explaining the new system, the best way for students to learn how it works is by implementing it as described in the previous section. Often times, the most challenging students will like this system the most. They can see how they are doing all the time and the idea of "points" is within their experience.

Using It as a Warmup/Do Now

Jim Peterson emphasizes the importance of beginning this system even before class officially begins by have a daily warmup or "do now" activity that students know they should do at the beginning of each class—reading their book, answering questions on the board, completing a math problem, etc. Teachers can expect their students to begin these initial activities two or three minutes before the bell rings, and at that time begin circulating and giving points (or taking them away from latecomers).

This process gets students focused immediately and can set a tone for the rest of the class period.

Weaning Students Off the System and Dealing with Reoccurrences

If this system is going well after a month of this kind of intensive effort, then it could be time to begin weaning students off the system. The teacher could begin telling students their point total fewer and fewer times. If that goes well, he could announce that, as students show that they are serious learners, he will take them off the points system—one at a time—and that they will get the maximum number of points automatically (with the caveat, of course, that he reserves the right to return them to the point system if they show that they are reverting to their prior behavior). At this time, it is not unusual to hear students asking each other, "Are you off the points system?"

or telling other students proudly, "I'm off the points system." This would be combined with the teacher sharing how pleased he is with the change.

If sometime after a student has already been removed from the point system but he is having a bad day, the teacher can give a warning that he risks being put back on it for that day. The first time I said that to a student, he responded with almost a sense of shame and said, "No, I don't need it, I can control myself and do my work without it!"

That can be a typical student response at that time—they now view the possibility of getting (or losing) points as something they don't want or need in order to be an academic student.

Of course, even with that realization, students might still have bad days. Individual students can be put back on the points system for a day, a week, or a month. Or, on a crazy day, the entire class can be placed back on it temporarily. But when that is done, many will feel the same way as that student—almost embarrassed that they need a carrots-and-sticks approach to behave and want to regain control of themselves as soon as possible.

Will there always be perfect behavior after you go off the system? No.

> But eighty percent on-task behavior that is intrinsically motivated is better than ninety-five percent on-task behavior that comes as a result of constant external control by the teacher.

Using the System Before a Class Gets Out of Control

One way to use this system effectively *before* a class gets out of control is by introducing it on the first day of school with any classes that *might* have challenging students. The teacher can explain the system, and then tell students that the shortest time it has ever taken for most students in a class to get off of it is two weeks, and that you hope they can break that record.

Especially at the beginning of a school year, when students are still a bit tentative, most classes will get off the system in "record time." As a result, the year gets off to a good start and knowledge of the system is in place to intervene before the class gets completely out of control.

For more information on Jim Peterson's system, you can go to http://larryferlazzo.edublogs.org/2009/02/23/have-you-ever-taught-a-class-that-got-out-of-control/ or go to Jim's site at www.AlphaMindCoaching.com. Jim's site not only gives more details on how to implement the system, but also provides the psychological reasons behind each step. You will also find a video of a teacher implementing the system in her classroom.

How Do You Help Students See Problems as Opportunities, Not Frustrations?

I constantly hear students making what sound like excuses: "This is too hard" or "I just don't get it" or "This is boring." Other than telling them that I know it's hard or boring and sometimes we have to do hard or boring things in our lives, I'm just not sure what to do.

Many years ago, I met a man who worked with Mahatma Gandhi in the struggle for India's independence. He said to me, "Larry, the key to Gandhi's success was that he looked at every problem as an opportunity, not as a pain."

Hearing that wise observation when I was so young, and truly understanding it, has enhanced my life immeasurably over the years. The question is: how can we help our students learn and apply the same concept?

Here are some ideas—both immediate and for "setting the stage." Two lesson plans are also included. The "Grit and Growth Mindset Lesson Plan" (page 71) is an appropriate followup to "The Brain as a Muscle Lesson Plan" found in Question 1 (see page 14).

Immediate Responses

Giving Students Feedback

Carol Dweck (2006), a Stanford professor, has researched and written a great deal about the importance of praising effort and not intelligence. Her research shows that by praising a student's persistence and the strategies they have used to overcome an obstacle, we reinforce a "growth mindset"—one in which students feel energized and knowledgeable about how to get beyond problems.

She contrasts the "growth mindset" with a "fixed mindset" that is promoted by praising intelligence ("You're so smart for getting that project done quickly"). Students with this kind of "fixed" perspective tend to want to look "smart" and value that image more than learning (Richardson, 2009). They tend to want to do easier work or might cheat so as to avoid making mistakes (Bronson, 2007) because making mistakes is not part of their self-image—they believe it may make them not look smart.

Dweck has done several experiments praising one group of students for their intelligence and the other for their effort—all with similar results. In one, both groups were given IQ tests and then, after receiving one or the other type of praise, were asked to solve difficult puzzles. The ones who were praised for their effort worked much harder at the puzzles than the ones praised for their intelligence—many of whom gave up in frustration. Students were then given an IQ test similar to the first one. In these second tests, the students who had been praised for their effort increased their score over the first time, whereas the other group scored lower than they had originally (Lehrer, 2009, October 22).

When trying to remember "in the moment" about what kind of feedback to give to students, it might be helpful to think of this guideline: "describe and/or question." Here are examples of praise that use this framework and will tend to develop more of a "growth" mindset:

- ◆ "Johnny, that was impressive that you did two drafts of that essay. What made you want to put that extra effort into it?"

- ◆ "You worked on that project for the entire period without getting distracted, just focusing on doing the best job you could. That's great!"

- "You really listened to the other questions that students were asking, and clearly tried to think of an original one. That really stood out!"

- (*To a student who might be facing behavior challenges*) "Frank, you were really focused on classwork today. Can you tell me what you did or thought to help yourself not get distracted? It would give me some ideas that I could suggest to other students."

What about a student who can easily and quickly do classwork? This is what Dweck says:

What about a student who gets an A without trying? I would say, "All right, that was too easy for you. Let's do something more challenging that you can learn from." We don't want to make something done quickly and easily the basis for our admiration (Dweck, 2007).

Setting the Stage

Helping Students See Their Own Growth

Dweck also suggests that creating opportunities for students to clearly see for themselves the growth in their own knowledge also advances a growth mindset.

As an example, this methodology is embedded in the Pebble Creek Labs (http://pebblecreeklabs.com/) curriculum used by Luther Burbank High School in Sacramento, California, and in many other schools across the country. Prior to beginning thematic units, a "Word Splash" (a list of key vocabulary) is shown to students. In small groups, students try to identify what each word means without the use of a dictionary, but the teacher does not provide the correct answer. Periodically, during the multiweek unit, students will revisit the word list and define the words based on what they learned through context clues during the course of unit activities.

Also, at the beginning of a unit, students might be asked to write everything they know about the topic they will be studying. The teacher collects the lists, and returns them at the end of the unit for students to see how little they knew a few weeks earlier compared to how much they know now.

Another way is to have students save writing samples during the course of the year, including one done right at the beginning of the term, and then have students assess them using an "Improvement Rubric." The "Improvement Rubric Lesson Plan" (page 76) provides a guide (and sample reproducibles) to implementing this idea.

Grit

Angela Duckworth, a professor at the University of Pennsylvania, has done research similar to that of Dweck. However, instead of using the terminology of "mindsets," Duckworth characterizes people as either having more "grit" or less "grit." She defines *grit* as perseverance toward achieving goals despite challenges and pitfalls along the way, and identifies the ability to ignore distractions as a key quality in developing grit (Duckworth, 2010).

Both Duckworth's and Dweck's work are incorporated into the "Grit & Growth Mindset Lesson Plan."

Grit & Growth Mindset Lesson Plan

Instructional Objectives

Students Will:

1. Learn about the psychological concepts of "mindsets" and "grit."

2. Demonstrate using reading strategies with a challenging text.

3. Develop strategies they can use to develop a "growth" mindset and more "grit."

Duration

One 55-minute class period and 30 minutes on the following day

Common Core English Language Arts Standards

Reading:

1. Determine central ideas or themes of a text and analyze their development; summarize the key supporting details and ideas.

Writing:

1. Write arguments to support claims in an analysis of substantive topics or texts, using valid reasoning and relevant and sufficient evidence.

Speaking & Listening:

1. Prepare for and participate effectively in a range of conversations and collaborations with diverse partners, building on others' ideas and expressing their own clearly and persuasively.

Language:

1. Demonstrate command of the conventions of standard English grammar and usage when writing or speaking.

2. Demonstrate command of the conventions of standard English capitalization, punctuation, and spelling when writing.

Materials

1. Student copies of the first two pages—or first eleven paragraphs—of "The Truth About Grit" (http://www.boston.com/bostonglobe/ideas/articles/2009/08/02/the_truth_about_grit/?page=1)

2. Student copies of Mindset chart (http://www.stanfordalumni.org/news/magazine/2007/marapr/images/features/dweck/dweck_mindset.pdf)

3. Student copies or Read Aloud of Michael Jordan, Jim Marshall, and Thomas Edison quotes on failure:

> **"I've missed more than 9000 shots in my career. I've lost almost 300 games. Twenty-six times I've been trusted to take the game winning shot and missed. I've failed over and over and over again in my life. And that is why I succeed."—Michael Jordan**

> **"While he really didn't want to come out for the second half, he remembered what his father taught him: Be responsible. If you make a mistake, you got to make it right. 'I realized I had a choice,' Marshall told me. 'I could sit in my misery or I could do something about it.' Marshall ended up playing one of his best halves ever. He hurried the passer into three interceptions and caused the fumble that Hall of Famer Carl Eller picked up and ran in for the winning touchdown." ("Disappointed Bush," 2008)**

> **"I have not failed, not once. I've discovered ten thousand ways that don't work."—Thomas Edison**

4. Challenges example (Figure 5.1, page 76)

5. Computer project and access to the Internet to show:

   ♦ "Michael Jordan 'Failure' Nike Commercial" (http://www.youtube.com/watch?v=45mMioJ5szc&feature=related. You can also find a the same video at a non-YouTube site that is unlikely to be blocked by school content filters: http://www.englishcentral.com/en/player/11260)

- ♦ "Jim Marshall's Wrong-Way Run in 1964" (http://www.youtube.com/watch?v=CocwASLXKlc)
- ♦ "Famous Failures" video (http://www.youtube.com/watch?v=dT4Fu-XDygw)

6. Overhead projector or poster to complete strategies chart.

Procedure

Note that "The Brain Is Like a Muscle Lesson Plan" (see page 14) should be done prior to this one.

First Day

1. Teacher explains that the class is going to learn about failures and making mistakes, and what we do afterward. Teacher asks, "If you have ever not accomplished something you wanted to achieve, or if you have ever made a mistake, raise your hand." Teacher then asks students to think about this question that is written on the board or overhead:

> Think about a time you didn't accomplish something you wanted to achieve, or think about a time you made a mistake. Please describe it.

Teacher asks students to respond to the prompt in writing. Then, after a minute, the teacher writes a second question on the board:

> How did it make you feel?

Teacher gives students a minute to respond in writing, then divides students into pairs to share their responses. Teacher calls on selected students to share their answers with the entire class.

2. Teacher asks students to raise their hands if they have heard of Michael Jordan, and asks students who know who he is to explain to the class. Teacher explains we are now going to learn what Michael Jordan thinks of failures and mistakes. Teacher shows the Nike commercial and repeats what Jordan said with it being shown on the overhead (see the Jordan quote above). Teacher asks students to take a minute and think about this question: "Why would he say that?" Teacher asks students to write down their answer and then share it with a partner. Teacher asks selected students to share their responses with the entire class.

3. Teacher shows the video of Jim Marshall running the wrong way, and then says he will read what Marshall said afterwards (see the quote above). (The teacher could skip this portion if you think it is redundant and to save time.)

4. Then the teacher reads the quote from Thomas Edison above.

5. Teacher shows "Famous Failures" video.

6. Teacher asks students to think what the "Famous Failures" video and the quotes from Jordan, Marshall, and Edison had in common, and to write down their answer. Students share in pairs, and then the teacher selects students to share with entire class.

7. Teacher explains that one of the things we are going to learn about today is a psychological concept called "grit." Teacher writes the word on the board and explains that grit is the ability to hang in there and get past setbacks when things don't go the way you hope—you don't let other things distract you from your goal.

8. Teacher explains that students are going to read the first two pages of an article about grit. They will take turns reading a paragraph to each other. For every two paragraphs, they will demonstrate a specific reading strategy in writing on the sheet. They should use each of the following reading strategies two times: make a connection, draw a picture to visualize, write a question, or write a summary. There are eleven paragraphs in the excerpt, and the teacher should model using the first three. The teacher reads the first paragraph and models writing a summary, and then models other strategies in the next two paragraphs. Students then divide into partners and do the assignment.

9. Teacher stops students once or twice to ask them to share what they wrote for each paragraph.

10. Teacher explains that a woman named Carol Dweck (remember her from the brain lesson?) calls grit something different—a "growth mindset." In a growth mindset, people think that when they fail at something they just need to try harder and get energized by it—mistakes are like puzzles. A person with a fixed mindset just thinks they don't have the ability to do it. In a growth mindset, we value hard work and effort.

11. Teacher reviews the Mindset chart on overhead—point by point. Teacher shares examples from his life to illustrate points, examples from the first part of the lesson, and/or asks students to share examples from their own lives that reflect different parts of the growth and fixed mindset.

12. Depending on how quickly the lesson goes, the teacher might not be able to complete reviewing the chart on the first day.

Second Day

1. The teacher completes reviewing the chart.

2. Next, the teacher explains that the students are going to list times when they feel challenged and we are going to discuss what strategies they might take to deal with them successfully so they can have a "growth" mindset. On an easel paper or on an overhead, the teacher writes down two columns. The left side is labeled "Challenge" and the right side is labeled "How to Overcome Them." The teacher can get the class started by listing some challenges (see Figure 5.1, page 76, for examples), and then asking the class to come up with some strategies to overcome them. Next, the teacher can ask students to work in partners to list more challenges and more strategies to overcome them. Students then share with the class, and teacher writes them down, creating a master chart to hang on the wall.

Assessment

1. The teacher could ask students to write a simple paragraph using the ABC or PQC format discussed in Question 1: How Do You Motivate Students? by asking them to answer the question: "What was the most interesting or important thing they learned from this lesson?" It should be simple to identify whether or not the students have annotated the "grit" article correctly with reading strategies.

2. If the teacher believes a more involved assessment is necessary, he can develop a simple rubric for appropriate for their classroom situation. Free online resources to both find premade rubrics and to create new ones can be found at http://larryferlazzo.edublogs.org/2010/09/18/the-best-rubric-sites-and-a-beginning-discussion-about-their-use/.

Possible Extensions/Modifications

1. Students create a poster showing one or two of the challenges and strategies to overcome them.

2. Teacher asks students to hold him accountable about praising effort and not intelligence. He makes it into a game: Every time they catch him doing it, the class receives some simple benefit.

3. After a teacher model, students write about something they are very good at now but in the past did not do well. They explain what they did to get to the point where they are now, and then share what they wrote with a partner and the class. As Dweck writes: "Such discussions encourage students not to be ashamed to struggle with something before they are good at it" (Dweck, 2010).

Ed Tech: Online Tests

Students could create an online test based on the information they learned in the lesson. Then their classmates could take one or two of them as an informal assessment. There are several free and easy-to-use tools to create these kinds of online tests. See http://larryferlazzo. edublogs.org/2008/05/22/the-best-ways-to-create-online-tests/ for more information.

Figure 5.1. Challenges and Responses

Challenge	Strategy to Overcome It
I'm having problems with math	Get a tutor
Too slow in basketball	Practice an outside shot
Don't understand words	Dictionary or reread, look for context clues
Boring lesson	Think of way to make it interesting

Improvement Rubric Lesson Plan

Instructional Objectives

Students Will:

1. Compare and assess, using an "improvement rubric," two pieces of similar work done with a substantial interval in between those times. For purposes of this lesson plan, it will be two essays—one done at the beginning of the year and one done closer to the end of the year. However, the interval could be shorter—one semester instead of one year.

2. Reflect on what areas of their writing they need to focus on improving the most.

3. Choose one of their essays to rewrite using their improvement rubric as a basis for revision.

Duration

Two 50-minute class periods

Common Core English Language Arts Standards

Reading:

1. Determine central ideas or themes of a text and analyze their development; summarize the key supporting details and ideas.

Writing:

1. Write arguments to support claims in an analysis of substantive topics or texts, using valid reasoning and relevant and sufficient evidence.

2. Produce clear and coherent writing in which the development, organization, and style are appropriate to task, purpose, and audience.

3. Develop and strengthen writing as needed by planning, revising, editing, rewriting, or trying a new approach.

Speaking & Listening:

1. Prepare for and participate effectively in a range of conversations and collaborations with diverse partners, building on others' ideas and expressing their own clearly and persuasively.

Language:

1. Demonstrate command of the conventions of standard English grammar and usage when writing or speaking.

2. Demonstrate command of the conventions of standard English capitalization, punctuation, and spelling when writing.

Materials

1. Student copies of the two pieces of work to be assessed.

2. Student copies of an Improvement Rubric. See Figure 5.2 (page 79) for an example. Teachers can create their own, emphasizing the areas they focused on in their instruction.

3. Student copies of reflection questions. See Figure 5.3 (page 80) for an example.

4. Overhead projector or document camera to show the rubric and questions.

Procedure

First Day

1. Teacher explains she is going to return to each student their first essay of the year and their last essay of the year (if students transferred into the class late, any earlier essay would suffice). Students will review each essay using the improvement rubric (Figure 5.2). Teacher reviews each point on the rubric.

2. Teacher distributes both the essays and rubric. Students work on them. After it appears that most students are completed, the teacher asks for students to look at the overhead, and she reviews the list of reflective questions (Figure 5.3, page 80). She distributes them for students to write their responses.

3. Teacher divides students into pairs and asks them to share their answers to the questions with their partner. After the sharing is complete, she asks selected students to share answers with the entire class, particularly focusing on the first question and drawing out from students that their hard work learning over the year resulted in a better essay.

4. Teacher explains that now students can choose one of their essays and revise it in light of their assessments to make it as good as they can.

5. Students began revising their essay.

Second Day

1. Students continue revising their essay until completed.

2. Depending on time available, students can be asked to complete a new assessment on their revised essay considering the same issues in the improvement rubric.

Assessment

Both students and the teacher can use the Improvement Rubric to assess their work.

Possible Extensions/Modifications

1. Students can read each other's essays (both originals and the revised one, and provide feedback based on the improvement rubric.

Ed Tech: Class Blogs

Students could type their essay in a Word document (useful for grammar and spelling assistance), then copy and paste it into a classroom blog. Classmates, after they see a teacher model, can then read and leave online comments about their classmates' essays. For more information, see http://larryferlazzo.edublogs.org/2008/05/19/part-two-of-the-best-sites-for-students-to-easily-create-display-online-projects/.

Figure 5.2. Improvement Rubric

ESSAY 1: "Why People Don't Help in a Crisis"				ESSAY 2: "Poets In the Kitchen"			
I opened my essay with an attention grabber (a hook)				I opened my essay with an attention grabber (a hook)			
1	2	3	4	1	2	3	4
I summarized the author's main points (They Say)				I summarized the author's main points (They Say)			
1	2	3	4	1	2	3	4
I wrote a thesis statement that stated whether I agreed/disagreed with the author (I Say)				I wrote a thesis statement that stated whether I agreed/disagreed with the author (I Say)			
1	2	3	4	1	2	3	4
I used at least one example from my life to support my opinion.				I used at least one example from my life to support my opinion.			
1	2	3	4	1	2	3	4
I used at least one example from another text, a movie, or an observation to support my opinion.				I used at least one example from another text, a movie, or an observation to support my opinion.			
1	2	3	4	1	2	3	4
I used at least one quotation from the article and explained it.				I used at least one quotation from the article and explained it.			
1	2	3	4	1	2	3	4
I organized my essay into paragraphs.				I organized my essay into paragraphs.			
1	2	3	4	1	2	3	4
I wrote a conclusion in which I summarized my main points and left the reader with something to think about.				I wrote a conclusion in which I summarized my main points and left the reader with something to think about.			
1	2	3	4	1	2	3	4

Created by Katie Hull and reprinted with her permission.

Figure 5.3. Improvement Rubric Questions

1. Look at the scores you gave yourself on both essays. Overall, which essay was your strongest? Why? What did you do to make it better?

2. Look at the scores on your strongest essay. What did you do well?

3. Look at the scores on your strongest essay. What are 3 things you need to get better at next year?

4. In what areas of your writing would you like your teacher next year to help you with?

What Are Some Ways You Can Get the Year Off to a Good Start?

It's that time again—a new year and new students! I sort of have a system to get started, and it seems to go okay, but I'm wondering if there are any better ways to begin a new school year?

As the old saying goes, you only have one opportunity to make a good first impression. The wisdom in that statement of the obvious makes it important to strategize carefully about the first week of school.

Teachers might be able to learn a helpful lesson from legendary San Francisco 49er football coach Bill Walsh. He began the now common practice among coaches to "script" the first fifteen to twenty-five plays his offense would run each game—no matter what. By using this method, his team was able to practice and perfect those plays during the week. Their success often created positive momentum that continued throughout the game (West Coast Offense, n.d.). Teachers could successfully apply the same reasoning to a first week of school.

This chapter lays out a specific schedule in the "First Week Unit Plan," which covers the first five days of a school year (geared toward an English class). More importantly, however, it discusses important characteristics most of those days should include (which might also be applied to *everyday* during the school year). Following the specific schedule in this lesson plan is much less important than carefully considering how to incorporate those key characteristics in a way that feels most comfortable to you and your students. Sample student handouts are also included.

More resources for getting the school year off to a good start can be found at http://larryferlazzo.edublogs.org/2009/08/09/answers-to-what-do-you-do-on-the-first-day-of-school/.

Criteria

What follows are the key characteristics that teachers might want to incorporate in every class every day, especially during the first week. Does that mean there is a problem if one is missed? No. These criteria, as is this entire book, is to be used as compass and not a road map. Keep them in mind as a planning tool. You will see that these criteria are incorporated during various times in the specific five-day schedule later in this chapter.

Building Relationships

Are you incorporating opportunities to build and strengthen your relationships with students, and for doing the same between students themselves? The importance of classroom relationships is discussed in the disruptive student chapter (see Question 3).

Set & Enforce High Expectations

Are you setting and enforcing high expectations, along with being realistic in your outlook and providing the necessary scaffolding so that students understand your expectations and have the tools to meet them? Some students may be coming to your classroom after years of being labeled "dumb" or of comfortably knowing how to "get by." It might take students awhile to become accustomed to higher standards, and some might need extra support to achieve them.

Engaging Lessons with the "Why?" Built into Them

Are your lessons engaging students, particularly in higher-order thinking skills, and is it clear to them why it is in their self-interest to learn what is being taught? See Question 8 on making lessons successful and Question 1 on student motivation for more specific ideas regarding these elements.

Assessments

Formative assessments are ongoing practices that help both the teacher and student evaluate and reflect on how they are both doing, and what changes either or both might need to make to become a more effective teacher and learner. These can be practices mentioned in other chapters in this book, such as providing student feedback (see Question 5), student summaries (see Question 9), and teacher observations (see Question 8). They differ from *summative* assessments such as midyear and final exams and state tests, which are primarily designed, at least theoretically, to determine more precisely what a student knows or doesn't know and often give him or her a formal grade or score.

Formative assessments are generally considered more useful to teachers. To quote Robert Marzano (2007), formative assessments "might be one of the more powerful weapons in a teacher's arsenal" (p. 13). Learn more about formative assessment at http://larryferlazzo.edublogs.org/2010/08/22/the-best-resources-for-learning-about-formative-assessment/.

Connecting with Parents

Having a good relationship with parents of students has been shown in numerous studies as benefiting student achievement (Ferlazzo & Hammond, 2009, p. 4). Teachers can develop and maintain this connection in several ways, including calling parents with positive news (as mentioned in previous chapters) and by having homework assignments that require student and parent interaction.

First Week Unit Plan

Instructional Objectives

Students Will:

1. Learn classroom rules, procedures and expectations.

2. Learn more about their teacher and classmates.

3. Begin reading a book of their choice and begin applying reading strategies.

4. Learn about research on self-control and the brain.

Duration

Five "double-block" periods (100 minutes each). Teachers can easily modify it for a single-period class.

Common Core English Language Arts Standards

Reading:

1. Determine central ideas or themes of a text and analyze their development; summarize the key supporting details and ideas.

Writing:

1. Produce clear and coherent writing in which the development, organization, and style are appropriate to task, purpose, and audience.

Speaking & Listening:

1. Prepare for and participate effectively in a range of conversations and collaborations with diverse partners, building on others' ideas and expressing their own clearly and persuasively.

2. Adapt speech to a variety of contexts and communicative tasks, demonstrating command of formal English when indicated or appropriate.

Language:

1. Demonstrate command of the conventions of standard English grammar and usage when writing or speaking.

2. Demonstrate command of the conventions of standard English capitalization, punctuation, and spelling when writing.

Materials

1. Document camera and computer project and Internet access, or overhead projector

2. Student copies of Student Questionnaire (Figure 3.2, page 55), Introduction Poster (Figure 6.1, page 91) and "Looking Back" form (Figure 6.2, page 92)

3. Poster paper and color markers

4. Premade seating chart designed to ensure ethnic and gender diversity

5. Binders or folders for each student

6. Student copies of a teacher-created "Book Pass" sheet

7. One-hundred high-interest books from a classroom or school library

8. A letter she writes to the class telling students about herself

9. Need materials from the "Brain Is Like a Muscle" Lesson Plan (see page 14) and from the Self-Control Lesson Plan (see page 57)

10. Two short passages that students will read as a fluency assessment. In addition to the passages themselves, the teacher will need a copy of the passage for each student that the teacher can use to mark (see http://larryferlazzo.edublogs.org/2010/08/22/measuring-reading-fluency/ for details)

Procedure

First Day

1. Teacher greets students individually at the door, asks them to look at the overhead seating chart to find their seats, and to immediately sit down and begin completing the Student Questionnaire (Figure 3.2, page 55).

2. After the bell rings, the teacher asks students to stop work on their questionnaire for a moment and lets them know they will have time to finish it later. After the teacher has all the students' attention, she can welcome them to the class. She explains that this is a college preparation class, and at the end of the year they will be ready to read just about anything. She then quickly explains a few key rules that are also written on the overhead:

   ◆ When I say "Can I have your attention?" that means I need everybody to stop what they're doing and look at me. I like to do a lot of small group work, and the more I believe I can get your attention when I need to, the more small group work we'll do.

   ◆ Be respectful—to each other, to me, to my stuff, and other student's stuff.

   ◆ We start class three minutes before the bell rings, so please be here on time. I'm excited to be your teacher, and I hope you'll want to be here in this class. I'll be sad if you're not here. As soon as you walk in, you should start reading your book.

   ◆ Eating can be a distraction, so I ask that you not eat food in the room. You're more than welcome, though, to come here during lunchtime to eat. As long as I don't see it or hear it, I usually don't notice if people are chewing gum. You can bring a water bottle to class, though, and drink water—only water—anytime you want.

3. The teacher then asks students to quickly introduce themselves to someone near them—saying their name, what school they went to the previous year, what they like to do for fun, where they live, and whether or not they

have any brothers or sisters (the teacher also posts these questions on the overhead). After doing that for three minutes, the teacher has them do the same thing with another student for three minutes more.

4. The teacher then quickly reviews a one-page syllabus that students can bring home to have parents sign.

5. The teacher then reviews her classroom management system, introducing the points system explained in Question 4, the out-of-control class chapter. The teacher emphasizes that she hopes to stop using it within weeks, if not sooner, as students show that they are as responsible as she expects them to be.

6. Then, students can go back to working on their questionnaire, making a simple "nameplate" that they can put on their desk for the first few days to help the teacher remember names, and write their name on a piece of paper they tape on a binder where they will be keeping their papers during the year, and which can be reused each year. During this time the teacher circulates and begins to have short conversations with students about what she sees they are writing down on their questionnaire.

7. After about fifteen minutes, the teacher passes out "Book Pass" sheets, which comes from Janet Allen (2000, p. 105). Teachers can create their own simple version that has one column for the titles of books, the next column for the name of the author, and the third column is where students rank them—1 means they are not interested in the book at all; 2 means they are "sort of" interested; and 3 means they are definitely interested. The teacher explains that she has sorted out 100 popular books, and that each student will receive some books, looks them over for a minute or so, record and rank them, and then pass them to the next person. After everyone has gone through all the books, each student will decide which one they want to check out. Prior to the distribution of books, the teacher asks students what they should look at during their minute, and draws out responses like looking at the cover, the back, and the first few pages of the book. In the middle of the book pass, the bell may ring for a break. When they return, the book pass continues for another twenty minutes or so and students pick their books. During this book-pass time, the teacher is circulating to see who is ranking which books high and low, and having brief conversations.

8. After about fifteen more minutes, students sign out the books they want to read and save their book-pass sheet in their binder or folder for future reference.

9. The teacher shows and reads a letter she has written to the class, and asks students, either as homework or during class time, to write a similar let-

ter to her (their letter provides more information and acts as aformative assessment of writing skills). Students can use what they wrote in their questionnaire, but should also add to it in the letter.

10. Next, the teacher models presenting an introduction using the form in Figure 6.1 (page 91). The teacher explains that students will be doing the same presentation, and the teacher makes a schedule for six students a day to present, beginning on the third day of school.

11. Students are given the rest of the period to work on their introduction posters while the teacher circulates throughout the room having individual conversations.

12. Later that day, and each day during the week, the teacher makes three or four calls to parents sharing how pleased she is to have their child in her class, and asking if they can offer her any advice based on their child's earlier school experience. She also explains that students will be asking them some questions about their high school experience as part of a future assignment. If their parents did not attend high school, students can be told to question other adults they know.

Second Day

1. Students should walk in three minutes before the bell rings and begin reading the book they checked out the previous day.

2. After fifteen minutes of reading, the teacher asks for the students' attention. She asks students to turn in the signed syllabus, and explains that she has one more piece of homework for them that will be due in three days. The teacher reviews the "Looking Back" survey (Figure 6.2, page 92) that lists questions students will ask their parents (it is based upon an idea written about by Robert Hampel [2010]). She explains that students, and the teacher, can learn from the experience of their parents, and that in three days students will share what they learned (it is also a good way for the teacher to learn a little more about the family background).

3. The teacher explains that while they finish their poster, she is going to call students one at a time to her desk so they can read to her. She shares that this will help her be a better teacher for them by knowing their reading strengths. While she listens, she asks that students remain on task.

4. Students are then given thirty minutes to complete their poster.

5. While they are working on their poster, students come up to the teacher's desk for three minutes each. She asks them a personal question about something they wrote in their questionnaire, and then has them read two passages to her for one minute each to assess their reading fluency. (This

reading assessment process is adapted from Pebble Creek Labs. For more details, see Mike Dunn's *Reading Fluency: What, Why, and How.*) The teacher continues to do this assessment with all students in the following days during their silent reading time at the beginning of class until all students are assessed.

6. The teacher then explains that in this class, students will become even better readers than they already are. She asks students to take out a piece of paper and fold it in half. Then she asks them to fold it in half again, and then unfold it. They should have four equal sections. On the overhead, she titles the first square "Why Do People Read." She asks students to take a minute or two to write down as many reasons as they can think of, and then has students share with a partner. The teacher then calls on students to contribute what they wrote and she writes them in her section and asks students to copy them down.

She then asks students to label the next section "Why Do You Read?" and asks students to write down their reasons. Students can choose from the first section, or write new reasons. After a minute, the teacher asks students to share what they wrote with a partner, but does not need to ask students to share with the entire class.

In the third box, the teacher writes "What Do Good Readers Do?" and asks students to answer it. After a minute or two, students share what they wrote with a partner, and then the teacher calls on students to share. The teacher writes what students suggest in her box, and then tells students she will make this section into a poster for the front of the classroom, and that new reading strategies will be added to it, too. She asks students to copy the list onto their sheets.

In the last box, the teacher writes "Are You a Good Reader? Why or Why Not? What is Easier About Reading for You? What is Harder About Reading for You?" The teacher asks students to complete that box, and tells students that the only person reading what they write will be the teacher. They will not be sharing it with other students.

The teacher then asks students to turn the paper over, and asks them to think of something they are good at now—playing basketball, cooking, playing a video game, etc. She wants them to write how they got good at it—it didn't just happen magically. What did they do to become good at whatever they chose to write about? After a minute or two, the teacher asks students to share with a partner and then with the class. Most students will probably say a lot of practice helped, and the teacher can emphasize that the same holds true with reading and writing. It does not matter if students are not good at it now—with practice they will become good at it.

The teacher then collects the papers. The information on them can provide very useful insights into the teacher's new students.

7. The teacher reminds students of the poster presentation schedule, and reviews basic presenting and listening etiquette.

8. After class, the teacher again makes a few phone calls to parents.

Third Day

1. During silent reading time, the teacher continues with the reading fluency assessments.

2. The teacher reminds students what they learned about being good listeners the previous day, and asks them to take out a sheet of paper. She explains that she wants each of them to write down the name of the student presenting, and at least one question they would like to ask the presenter. After the student presents, he/she will call on two or three students to ask their questions.

3. After three students present (there is nothing more deadly than an endless string of student presentations, which is why they are limited to three in a row), the teacher models how a cloze (a fill-in-the-blank passage) is completed. Students are then given two clozes (teacher or school created) to complete as part of their formative assessment.

4. The lesson on "The Brain Is Like a Muscle" (page 14) is begun, but stopped to give three students time to present.

5. Three students present.

6. After the class, the teacher again makes a few phone calls to parents.

Fourth Day

1. During silent reading time, the teacher continues with the reading fluency assessments.

2. Three more students present.

3. "The Brain Is Like a Muscle" lesson is completed.

4. Three more students present.

5. After the class, the teacher again makes a few phone calls to parents.

Fifth Day

1. During silent reading time, the teacher continues with the reading fluency assessments.

2. Three more students present.

3. The teacher asks students to complete a short self-reflection and writes on the board:

   ◆ What things do you like about the school and your classes?

   ◆ What are your concerns about the school and your classes?

   She asks students to write answers to those questions, have them share what they wrote with a partner, and then have a few students share with the entire class before turning in the sheet to the teacher.

4. She then asks students to take out their completed "Looking Back" survey (Figure 6.2, page 92) from home. She asks students to review the survey and pick out one short piece—no more than one sentence—of good advice in it. Then, she explains that students are going to walk around and ask five other students to share what they chose. Students will write down in the back of their survey sheet the five pieces of advice they learn.

5. When completed, students will return to their sheets and choose the piece of advice they like best, write it on a piece of poster paper, and quickly illustrate it. At the bottom of their poster they also need to write a sentence explaining why they chose that particular piece of advice. The teacher will collect the posters to post on the classroom wall.

6. The teacher then does the marshmallow lesson (see page 57) in Question 3, the disruptive student chapter chapter.

7. Three more students present.

8. After the class, the teacher again makes a few phone calls to parents.

Assessment

1. Teachers can use the assessment suggestions in the previous lesson plans and/or create a more detailed rubric appropriate for their classroom situation.

Figure 6.1. Introduction Poster

1. Write your name on the board.

2. My name is _____.

3. This is _____.

    It is important to me because _____.
(Please bring at least three objects.)

4. Present your "Who Am I?" Poster with pictures and sentences. The categories are:

    ♦ My Loves (I love _____ because _____.)

    ♦ My Worries (I worry about _____ because _____.)

    ♦ My Sadnesses (I feel sad when _____ because _____.)

    ♦ My Hopes and Dreams (I hope _____ because _____.)

    ♦ My Successes (I'm good at _____
    because _____.)

You should have at least two items in each category.

Figure 6.2. "Looking Back" Survey

Student Name _____

Parent/Guardian/Grandparent/Older Sibling _____

"LOOKING BACK" SURVEY

1. What were the two or three most important things you learned in high school? Why were they so important? How did you learn them?

2. If you could travel back in time, what would you change—in your own behavior or in the school itself—to make your high school experience better?

3. What teacher did you learn the most from? Why do you think you learned the most from him/her?

4. What advice would you give to a student to help him/her have a good high school experience?

Signed _____

What Can You Do to Help Keep Your Students—and Yourself—Focused at the End of the School Year?

State testing is done, the weather is getting nicer, and we are all getting spring fever. There are six or seven weeks left of school and students are easily distracted. It's even hard for me to stay focused. I don't just want to "coast." What can I do?

Those last few weeks of school can be challenging, and it is understandable that both students and teachers are tempted to "slack off" a bit. However, it is important for our students' futures that we actually "step up" the quality and intensity of what is happening in our classrooms during that time period.

Nobel Prize winner Daniel Kahneman tells about an experiment done in the 1990s when two groups of patients were given colonoscopies. One group "finished" when the procedure was completed, whereas the other stayed a short while believing the procedure was continuing but in fact it had ended, so the pain was gone or reduced dramatically. The second group described the procedure afterward as much less painful than the first one, even though both groups had recorded similar levels of pain during the procedure—except for the extra time for the second group (Kahneman, 2010). Kahneman uses this example to explain that we have an "experiencing self" and a "remembering self."

> **The "remembering self" is comprised of the one or two "peak" moments we have had in a situation combined with how it ends (this is known as the "Peak/End Rule"). It is the remembering self that tends to stick with us, and on which we use to base future decisions.**

In other words, what occurs in the final weeks in your classes will have a huge influence on how students feel about—and make future decisions related to—learning, schooling, the subject you are teaching, future teachers (and how they might feel about future male or female teachers, depending on your gender), showing leadership in a class, etc.

This time provides you the opportunity to help your students finish strongly and to even include a "peak" or two.

This chapter shares several ideas—in a quasi-chronological order—on how teachers can work with students to maximize the use of this period of time. First, there is a suggestion about how to introduce this "strong finish." Next, there are a few ideas for engaging projects students can work on during the bulk of the time. Then, there are specific suggestions on how to use the final few days of the school term effectively. Lesson plans are included.

There is an additional section with suggestions to teachers on how they can maintain their focus near the end of a long school year.

Introducing the Idea of a Strong Finish

There is a lesson plan later in this chapter that provides a guide on introducing to students the idea of a "strong finish." Part of it includes having students answer two questions:

- What are three things you can do to help finish the school year strong academically? *try hard, give it a try, listen, do my best*

- What is one thing you can do to help your classmates finish the year strong academically? *Kindness, help*

The lesson works best if you have already used the "Goal-Setting Lesson Plan" in the Question 1 (see page 19) and can refer back to it. However, if you have not yet taught that lesson, you might want to consider incorporating some of its parts that speak to why it is important to set goals.

Engaging Student Projects

Students' Own Unit Plan

— 200/animal unit

Having small groups of students identify a topic in which they have a high-degree of interest, prepare a full-fledged unit instructional plan on the topic, and then teach a portion to the class, can be a strong motivator near the end of the school year.

The lesson plan in this chapter includes having students use the higher-order thinking instructional methods described in Question 10 and elsewhere in this book—inductive learning, clozes, and think-alouds. Another teaching strategy that can develop higher-order thinking skills is a sequencing exercise similar to a "sentence scramble" (discussed in the Question 13: How Can You Best Use Learning Games in the Classroom?), but done with a longer passage. Figure 7.1 (page 96) provides a sample sequencing activity. When students cut out the strips and place them in order, they should also be highlight the clue words that led them to put the strip in the sequence they are using. A variation of this sequencing strategy is providing students with a series of questions along with answers that are "mixed up." Students then have to connect the correct answers with the appropriate questions and highlight the clue words.

Of course, students should not be asked to use any instructional strategy that they have not seen modeled by the teacher multiple times during the year. So if inductive learning, clozes, think-alouds, or sequencing activities have not been used previously, now is not the time to begin. Students should use whatever typical engaging instructional methods had been previously used in the class.

Field Trip—Real and/or Virtual

— 200 trip

A local, or not-so-local, field trip can always be an energizer at the end of the year. Learning activities in the days leading up to the trip—specifically related to the trip—and a reflective activity following it can provide a good week's worth of engagement.

Logistically and financially, though, sometimes a "real" field trip can be challenging. If that is the case, thanks to Web 2.0 technology you can now have students create their own virtual field trips on the Web. There are many free websites that will let users easily create virtual field trips (see http://larryferlazzo.edublogs.org/2009/09/08/the-best-sites-where-students-can-plan-virtual-trips/). Students can use these applications to visit places online and describe them, and show them to their classmates.

Life cycle of animal kingdoms

Figure 7.1. Sequencing Activity Example

1. George left the farm when he was young and fought for the British in the French and Indian War. He left the army after his brother died and George inherited the farm and home.

2. George Washington is famous in the United States and in many parts of the world. He is known as "The Father of Our Country." His picture is on the dollar bill and our capital city is named after him.

3. George Washington died in 1799.

4. GEORGE WASHINGTON'S LIFE

5. His father died when he was eleven, and a few years later he went to live with his half-brother Lawrence at Mount Vernon, a big farm.

6. George Washington was born February 22, 1732 in Virginia.

7. When the American colonists decided to fight for independence from England, they appointed George as general in charge of all their soldiers because of his experience in the British army.

8. After the colonists won their independence, George became president for eight years. He refused to stay as president any longer, and he and his wife, Martha, retired to Mount Vernon.

Correct sequence: 4, 2, 6, 5, 1, 7, 8, 3 (This is obviously not shared with students until after they are finished.)

Other Technology Projects

Whether it is incorporating technology in their own unit plans, creating virtual field trips, or creating other online projects for "authentic audiences"—where people other than the teacher can see and comment on it—the end of the school year can be an excellent time to engage students with technology.

Question 12 on incorporating technology in the classroom is filled with examples, and the author's blog is continually updated with new ideas and applications.

computer lab / skills

Other Cooperative Learning Projects

Question 11 on cooperative learning provides resources and ideas about cooperative learning activities, including problem-based and project-based learning. If a student-created unit plan does not sound like a good idea for some reason, other cooperative-learning activities are good alternatives.

The Last Few Days of School

The last two days of school are a different "kettle of fish" that may require special handling. Suggestions for what to do during these times are covered in two sections in this chapter—one is called "Celebrate and Appreciate" and the other is "Evaluate and Agitate."

A common theme during this time could be titled "Placate and Vegetate." Using this strategy, the teacher puts on a movie, sets out games for students to play, or allows them to listen to music and chat. Everybody pretty much just counts down the minutes. We do our students a disservice, especially in urban schools, when we choose this category. For many of our students, school provides constancy and order in otherwise chaotic lives. These days are our last opportunity to honor their work and help them prepare for what might be a boring two-and-half months at home. For many, those months will be followed by a major transition to another grade, another school, or another city—sometimes without a lot of family support.

Here are some ideas about what we can do instead.

Celebrate and Appreciate

As mentioned previously, one time where research says rewards do not diminish intrinsic motivation is when people receive recognition when they do not expect it. Even the most aloof teenager enjoys getting a certificate recognizing him/her for some accomplishment (it is easy to make free, good-looking certificates; see http://larryferlazzo.edublogs.org/2009/05/16/the-best-ways-to-make-awards-certificates-online/).

1st grade awards

Teachers probably want to think strategically about which students would prefer receiving serious awards, and which ones would enjoy getting more humorous ones.

Agitate and Evaluate

Community organizers often talk about the difference between "irritation" and "agitation." I am irritating you if I am challenging you to do something about a topic *I'm* interested in. On the other hand, I'm agitating you if I'm pushing you to do something about a topic *you're* interested in.

We want to do as much agitating as we can in the classroom, especially during the last two days of school.

There are a few things that are likely to grab student interest during the last two days of school—turning the tables and "grading" the teacher, having them talk about themselves, and giving students a head start on getting a good grade in their next year's class.

Student Evaluations of Teachers

Student evaluations of teachers can be invaluable sources of helpful feedback. Countless studies confirm this fact on the college/university level (Doyle, n.d.). Similar studies, though far fewer, have reached the same conclusions for K-12 teachers (Peterson & Stevens, 1988). The school district in Boston, with the cooperation of the teachers union, has even be made it a districtwide policy to have students evaluate their teachers (Stickgold, 2010).

Figures 7.2 and 7.3 (page 100) are examples of two different kinds of evaluations. Maintaining the anonymity of the evaluators is, of course, an important part of the process to ensure candid feedback.

One way to help ensure that students take these evaluations seriously might be by demonstrating that *you* do. For example, I always let students know that I will be sharing the results—"warts" and all—with other colleagues at school, as well as publishing them in my blog.

Community organizers often talk about the difference between "opinion" and "judgment." Opinion is something you develop on your own—it's "untested." Judgment, on the other hand, is the result of interaction with others—where you allow yourself to hear what others might have seen that you did not. One way to help students learn this difference is by having students share what they wrote with each other—perhaps in a "speed-dating" process described in previous lesson plans—and giving them the opportunity to revise their evaluations afterwards if they so desire.

Figure 7.2. ARW Class Evaluation Form

Please do not put your name on this form. Circle one answer

1. In this class, I learned… *some   a lot   little*

2. I tried my best in this class… *a lot of the time   all the time   some of the time*

3. My favorite unit was… *New Orleans   Natural Disasters   Latin Studies   Mandela   Mt. Everest Jamaica*

4. My least favorite unit was… *New Orleans   Natural Disasters   Latin Studies   Mandela   Mt. Everest Jamaica*

5. As a teacher, I think Mr. Ferlazzo is… *okay   good   excellent   bad*

6. Did you feel that Mr. Ferlazzo was concerned about what was happening in your life? *yes   no*

7. Mr. Ferlazzo is patient… *some of the time   a lot of the time   all of the time*

8. Did you like this class? *yes   no*

9. Would you want to take another class taught by Mr. Ferlazzo? *yes   no*

10. What was your favorite activity in this class? *practice reading   data sets   make-and-breaks   read-alouds   clozes   writing essays   working in groups*

Please write your answers to the following two questions:

11. What could you have done to make this class a better learning experience?

12. What could Mr. Ferlazzo have done to make this class a better learning experience?

Figure 7.3. Theory of Knowledge Class Evaluation

1. What are the two or three most important things you learned in this class?

2. What did you like about this class or how it was taught?

3. How do you think this class could be improved?

4. What grade would you give Mr. Ferlazzo as a teacher? What do you think he does well? What do you think he could improve?

5. Are there ways you think that what you learned in this class will help you in the future? If so, what are they?

Although it is not quite the same as an evaluation, teachers can also gain useful feedback by having students write letters to students who will be taking the same class the following year. Figure 7.4 is an example of this assignment.

Figure 7.4. Letter to ~~Ninth graders~~ Kindergarteners

50 Points

Please write a letter to the incoming ninth graders who will be taking this class next year. Please describe what they will be learning in this class and give them some tips for being successful. You may also want to give them some information about Burbank, the Information Technology Small Learning Community, the teachers they will have, and any advice on how to have a good ninth grade year.

Talking About Themselves   *Letter to 2nd grade teacher*

T.S. Eliot wrote, "To make an end is to make a beginning." So, as another step toward thinking about the year to come, teachers could have students draw and write a metaphor or simile of themselves (I am like a _____ because _____) that can be given to their next year's teacher. You can explain that this will be the first impression their new teacher will have of them. This is one more way students can reinforce a positive self-image. It also opens the way for the student and new teacher to make an early personal connection when they meet in the fall.

As in most student projects, it will be important for the teacher to demonstrate a model. In addition, having students share their creations with their classmates could be another nice year-end closing activity.

Getting a Head Start on Next Year's Class

In low-income communities, the "summer slide" accounts for as much as 80% of the achievement gap (Toppo, 2010). Students who do not read during that time fall three months behind their middle-class peers each year.

One way to combat that loss is to share with students the impact their not reading can have on their future, and encourage them to take steps to ensure these negative consequences do not happen to them. I have students check books out of my classroom library (and have lost very few books because of it over the years). Taking a field trip to the local library is another option.

Ideally, teachers can make arrangements with their next year's teachers to provide some kind of extra credit to students for their summertime reading. One option is to have students meet with you when the next school year begins to answer a few questions about the book to ensure that they actually read it. Then you can communicate that information to their new teacher.

How Can Teachers Stay Energized?

What follows are a few ideas that are modified versions of what community organizers are often urged to do when they are feeling "burned out":

♦ *Work fewer hours:* By this time of the year, "throwing time" at school doesn't pay dividends. Cutting back on outrageous work hours per week can often result in feeling more energized in the classroom.

♦ *Read a stimulating book:* Finding an intellectually stimulating book (or article) on teaching and learning might get you excited to try out some new things—even though it's at the end of the year.

Ed Tech: Watch an Intellectually Stimulating Video on the Web

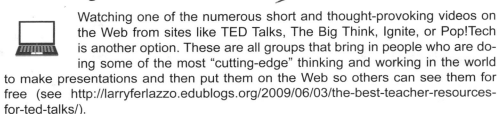

Watching one of the numerous short and thought-provoking videos on the Web from sites like TED Talks, The Big Think, Ignite, or Pop!Tech is another option. These are all groups that bring in people who are doing some of the most "cutting-edge" thinking and working in the world to make presentations and then put them on the Web so others can see them for free (see http://larryferlazzo.edublogs.org/2009/06/03/the-best-teacher-resources-for-ted-talks/).

♦ *Write something useful for other teachers:* Whether it's a blog post or a lesson plan to be shared (or something else), forcing yourself to craft something public can keep your mind sharp.

♦ *Make a point to eat lunch—individually—with teachers you don't know well, but are impressed with:* It can be energizing to meet with another teacher and learn why they chose this profession, what they've learned about teaching and learning, what gives them energy, and just their "story."

Ed Tech: Develop a Personal Learning Network Using Social Media

Thousands of teachers across the world use tools like Facebook, Twitter, and blogs to connect with each other. Whether it's at the end of the year, or at the beginning, developing these kinds of virtual relationships can be energizing and professionally helpful. You can find resources to get started at http://larryferlazzo.edublogs.org/2010/12/21/the-best-guides-for-helping-teachers-develop-personal-learning-networks/.

"Strong Finish" Lesson Plan

Instructional Objectives

Students Will:

1. Learn what class plans are for the final six weeks of school.

2. Identify ways they can motivate themselves and help their classmates to work hard during this time.

Duration

Forty minutes, assuming that the goal-setting lesson (see page 19) was done earlier. If not, the teacher might want to incorporate into this lesson plan some aspects of that lesson plan. If that is done, this lesson could last between one and two 55-minute class periods.

Common Core English Language Arts Standards

Writing:

1. Produce clear and coherent writing in which the development, organization, and style are appropriate to task, purpose, and audience.

Speaking & Listening:

1. Prepare for and participate effectively in a range of conversations and collaborations with diverse partners, building on others' ideas and expressing their own clearly and persuasively.

2. Adapt speech to a variety of contexts and communicative tasks, demonstrating command of formal English when indicated or appropriate.

Language:

1. Demonstrate command of the conventions of standard English grammar and usage when writing or speaking.

2. Demonstrate command of the conventions of standard English capitalization, punctuation, and spelling when writing.

Materials

1. Document camera/overhead projector or whiteboard

2. Model teacher poster on goals

3. Paper and color markers for students to make their own posters

4. If elements of the previous goal-setting lesson and lesson on "grit" are to be included, then those materials will also be needed

Procedure

First Day

1. Teacher writes *Grit* on the overhead, and asks students to write down what that means to them. (If the class has done that lesson plan—see Question 5—they might remember.) Teacher has students share what they wrote with a partner, and then asks some students to share with the class. The teacher either reminds students (if they had done the lesson plan previously) or tells them for the first time about studies that have shown that grit—or persistence—is a key quality of people who are successful.

2. Teacher congratulates students on the good work they have done so far this year and explains that the remaining few weeks will be an opportunity for them to show that they have "grit." Teacher shares—in an enthusiastic way—what the class will be doing in the remaining weeks. (These should be exciting and engaging projects. This chapter recommends student-created units, field trips—real or virtual—and other technology projects. There are, however, countless other cooperative learning activities that could be other alternatives.)

3. The teacher could consider saying that to support helping students develop their "grit" capacity, he is going to place a heavier weight on grades that students earn over the next few weeks than from the first few weeks of the semester. Another alternative is doing this lesson a few weeks earlier at the beginning of the last grade quarter (if the school is on a quarter system) and telling students that all of them will begin the quarter with an A. (I know some teachers just continue student grades from the first quarter of a semester, but I have always thought that a "new beginning" worked better, while informing students that I would place a heavier weight on the grade they earned in second quarter.)

4. Teacher tells students he wants them to answer two questions, which he shows on the overhead or whiteboard:

    ♦ What are three things you can do to help finish the school year strong academically?

    ♦ What is one thing you can do to help your classmates finish the year strong academically?

The teacher could offer a suggestion or two, such as "continue reading every night."

5. After several minutes, the teacher asks students to share what they wrote with a partner. Then he asks some students to share with the class.

6. Next, the teacher explains that he wants students to pick their best response to the first question (or they could borrow from someone else, if they like that idea better). Then they are going to make a poster. One half of the poster will be labeled "What Can I Do to Finish the School Year Strong Academically?" with their answer below it along with an illustration. The other half will be labeled "How Will I Help My Classmates Finish the Year Strong Academically?" with their answer below it along with an illustration. The teacher could show a model poster.

7. Student work on their poster for twenty minutes.

8. The teacher has two options:

   ♦ Divide students up into two lines facing each other and have them show and read their posters to each other in a "speed-dating" style that was described in previous lesson plans.

   ♦ Have students put their posters on the walls, and have students walk around looking at them for a few minutes. Students could be asked to take notes on which ideas they liked the most, and then have a short class discussion.

Assessment

The lesson and instructions are fairly simple, and it should be easy to determine if students performed the work. If the teacher does think a more involved assessment is necessary, she can develop a simple rubric for appropriate for their classroom situation. Free online resources to both find premade rubrics and to create new ones can be found at http://larryferlazzo.edublogs.org/2010/09/18/the-best-rubric-sites-and-a-beginning-discussion-about-their-use/.

Possible Extensions/Modifications

The teacher could ask students to respond to the two questions by writing paragraphs using the ABC format described in Question 1 (see Figure 1.4, page 18).

Ed Tech: Goal-Setting Applications

There are many free and easy online goal-setting applications where users can identify goals and track their progress toward achieving them. If students are regularly going to the computer lab, using one of these sites for a few minutes could be a useful motivating tool. Two sites to consider are LifeTango (http://www.lifetango.com/) and eLifeList (http://www.elifelist.com/index.php). You can read more about them here http://larryferlazzo.edublogs.org/2007/11/02/student-goals/.

Student-Created Unit Lesson Plan

Instructional Objectives

Students Will:

1. Create a unit plan on a topic of their choice using instructional strategies that have been used in the classroom during the year.
2. Teach one of the lessons from their unit plan to the class.

Duration

Ten to fifteen class periods

Common Core English Language Arts Standards

Reading:

1. Determine central ideas or themes of a text and analyze their development; summarize the key supporting details and ideas.

Writing:

1. Produce clear and coherent writing in which the development, organization, and style are appropriate to task, purpose, and audience.

Speaking & Listening:

1. Prepare for and participate effectively in a range of conversations and collaborations with diverse partners, building on others' ideas and expressing their own clearly and persuasively.

2. Adapt speech to a variety of contexts and communicative tasks, demonstrating command of formal English when indicated or appropriate.

Language:

1. Demonstrate command of the conventions of standard English grammar and usage when writing or speaking.

2. Demonstrate command of the conventions of standard English capitalization, punctuation, and spelling when writing.

Materials

1. Student copies of lesson preparation materials (samples are in Figures 7.5 to 7.9, page 109 to page 111)

2. Overhead project/document camera and/or easel paper

3. Student copies of handouts created by students

Procedure

First Day

1. Teacher asks students to think about, and write down, the three things they are most interested in—that really "gets their juices flowing." Teacher asks students to share what they wrote with a partner, and then asks some students to share with the class.

2. Teacher explains that students will be able to work in pairs or groups of three to develop a unit plan to teach about a topic that they are really, really interested in. The teacher says that he has to approve the topic, but that he will be very, very flexible. (Note that the sample student handouts in this chapter are directed toward students completing an ethnic studies project. However, these samples can be easily modified to talk about any topic students want to teach, or any period in world history, etc.)

3. The teacher quickly summarizes what will be part of each unit plan using Figure 7.5 (page 109) as an example. Of course, teachers can modify any elements, and can add activities such as a learning game or a PowerPoint presentation. The teacher explains that he will be providing detailed guidelines about how to prepare the unit plan and teach the lesson.

4. The teacher should give students time to determine their groups and topic while the teacher circulates and answers questions. The teacher explains that any topic is subject to his approval. Each group should write the students' names and topic on a sheet of paper.

5. After that is completed, the teacher can review the timeline with students—how many days in the computer lab, how much time for practice, when the lessons will need to be taught, etc. The timeline will depend on

which activities the teacher wants in the lesson plan. Developing a data set, cloze, and sequencing sheet could take three to four class periods in the computer lab.

Second, Third, Fourth, & Fifth Days

1. The teacher should review the instructions for one activity each day to minimize student confusion.

2. Students work on preparing their materials. They should give the teacher individual copies of the hand-outs they will use in the lessons so that the teacher can make copies.

Sixth Day

1. Students prepare their lesson plan and practice teaching in their small groups.

Seventh, Eighth, Ninth, & Tenth Days

1. Students should teach their lessons—probably not more than two lessons each day. The teacher should have other activities prepared if there is any leftover time. Another option is to have students teach their lessons in small groups instead of to the entire class.

2. After each lesson, the teacher can lead a brief class discussion on what the student teachers did well and what they could have done better.

Assessment

1. Each element of this assignment is very specific, and it should be relatively simple to determine whether or not students completed them. If the teacher thinks a more involved assessment is necessary, he can develop a simple rubric appropriate for his classroom situation. Free online resources to both find premade rubrics and to create new ones can be found at http://larryferlazzo.edublogs.org/2010/09/18/the-best-rubric-sites-and-a-beginning-discussion-about-their-use/.

2. Teachers can also ask students to write an answer to the question: What did you learn about teaching and being a teacher?

Possible Extensions/Modifications

Each student lesson could be videotaped for review and self-critique by each small group.

Figure 7.5. Ethnic Studies Project

1. You will choose to work in a group of three to develop a mini-unit on the literature, history, and/or achievements of one of these ethnic groups:

   ◆ Hmong

   ◆ African American

   ◆ Latino

   ◆ Pacific Islander

   ◆ Mien

2. Each mini-unit must include a:

   ◆ Cloze with at least ten "blanks"

   ◆ A Sequencing Sheet with at least eight sections

   ◆ Data set with at least three categories and at least fifteen examples

3. You will teach one of these lessons to the class.

4. These units will be taught in classes throughout the school next year!

5. All three lessons must be completed by Friday, May 14th.

6. We will be in the computer lab for four periods between now and then.

7. Your final project should consist of these sections in this order:

   ◆ Cover sheet with your names & ethnic group

   ◆ Cloze and answer sheet

   ◆ Make and Break and answer sheet

   ◆ Data set and answer sheet

   ◆ Lesson plan for the lesson you are going to teach, including who is going to say and do what. All people in your group must speak.

Figure 7.6. Cloze Instructions

♦ Pick a passage related to your chosen ethnic group and seems interesting. It should have more than one paragraph, but not be longer than one page.

♦ Copy and paste the original passage onto a Word document and cite the author. This will be your answer key.

♦ Copy and paste it again on another Word document. You will make this copy into a cloze.

♦ Read the passage carefully and select ten words that you will replace with blanks. Be sure that there are clue words for each blank. Circle the clue words on your answer sheet.

♦ Do not have a blank in the first or last sentence of the passage and do not have more than one blank in the same sentence.

Place the answer words on the bottom of the page. Be sure that they are not in the correct order.

Figure 7.7. Sequencing Sheet Instructions

1. Choose a passage that is chronological (a story, biography, or history) and related to your chosen ethnic group. Make sure the passage is no longer than a page-and-half and can easily be divided into at least eight sections.

2. Copy and paste the original passage onto a Word document and cite the author and source. This will be your answer key.

3. Copy and paste it again on another Word document. You will make this copy into your Sequencing Sheet.

4. Read the passage carefully and divide it into eight sections. Be sure that there are clue words for each section. Circle the clue words on your answer sheet. Number each section.

5. Copy and paste the sections so that they are not in order and leave space between each one because students will be cutting-them.

Figure 7.8. Data Set Instructions

1. Pick at least three categories about your ethnic group (history, music, sports, famous people, literature, etc.).

2. Each group member should focus on one category.

3. Each group member should find at least five passages of no more than five sentences each that relate to their category (think of all the data sets you've read this year).

4. Your group is creating one data set with three categories. Type in or copy and paste all fifteen exemplars so they are mixed together (think of all the data sets you've read this year). Number each exemplar.

5. List the names of your three categories at the top of the data set.

6. On another Word document, prepare an answer sheet listing each category and the numbers that fit into it.

Figure 7.9. Lesson Plan Instructions

1. You can choose to teach either the cloze, sequencing activity, or data set. You only have to teach the class or a small group. You will receive extra credit if you teach the make-and-break or the data set.

2. Decide how you are going to introduce your lesson. How are you going to grab their attention?

3. Think about what tools your students will need.

4. Do you want students to do the assignment alone, with a partner, or both?

5. What are the specific things you want your students to do? How are you going to communicate that to them—on the overhead, verbally, on the whiteboard?

6. How much time are you going to give them to complete the assignment?

7. How are you going to support students while they are completing the assignment?

8. Are you going to have them share their answers with someone else before they share with the entire class or the other students in their small group?

9. What questions are you going to have students answer to the whole class or entire small group, and how are you going to get them to respond (are you going to call on individuals)?

10. How will you end the lesson?

Part II

Classroom Instruction

What Are the Best Things You Can Do to Maximize the Chances of a Lesson Being Successful?

My lessons tend be pretty uneven. Sometimes, they seem to hit a home run. Other times, they're stinkers. And often I can't tell what made the difference!

There are obviously many, many things that teachers can do to maximize the chances of an individual lesson going well. This chapter shares just a few elements that research (and personal experience) tend to say are important. It is not designed as a universal checklist for teachers to ensure that every lesson they do includes every characteristic listed. On occasion, some successful lessons might not include any of these qualities. Other times, some duds might include most of them. So, the question is not:

Do all of my lessons have all of these characteristics all of the time?

Instead, it is designed more as a guide for teachers to periodically consider and ask themselves this question:

Do most of my lessons have several of these characteristics most of the time?

If the answer is yes to the second question, the studies cited suggest that you are more likely to consistently have successful lessons—ones where not only have *you taught* what you wanted, but students *have actually learned it*, too.

Of course, in addition to the points listed here, the ideas described in many of the other chapters in this book, particularly those concerning student motivation and building relationships, are critical, too. Without those, these ideas are just the "words" without the "music."

The eleven elements discussed below are not listed in any kind of chronological order. Even ideas from the introductions and reflection sections can be applied throughout any particular lesson. For example, creating novelty, identifying opportunities for students to transfer what they are learning to other areas, and activating background knowledge do not have to be—and should not be—limited to only the introduction period of a lesson. The same holds true for reflecting, reviewing, and summarizing, which can all occur at various points during the lesson and not just at the end.

Elements to Consider, Including in Lesson Plans

Strategic Introductions

A "strategic introduction" to a lesson includes several aspects.

Novelty

Our brains are wired to respond to something new—a survival legacy of our ancestors who had to be acutely aware of any change in their environment (Wolfe, 2001, p. 82). You are more likely to grab students' attention by introducing information, a topic, or a lesson in a different way.

This does not mean that a teacher has to get dressed-up in a costume. It could be something as simple as:

♦ Writing an unexpected word on the board and asking students to write its definition (as in the lesson where students were asked to write what they thought "self-control" meant; see page 57). Asking students to respond to a thought-provoking question that connects to their personal experience (as in the mindset lesson plan where they were asked to write about a failure or mistake; see page 71).

♦ Placing a group of intriguing uncaptioned photos on the wall, or a multicolored list of curious sounding words without their definition (also known as a "Word Splash") that are related to an upcoming lesson, two or three days prior to a lesson.

- Showing a one- or two-minute video scene that stands out. For example, in a Pebble Creek Labs lesson (http://pebblecreeklabs. com/), prior to telling students they will be learning about Nelson Mandela, a short clip is shown of hundreds of thousands of people greeting and following him when he is released from prison. Students are then asked:

   What kinds of events would make everybody in a country stop what they were doing?

Relevance

Judy Willis, neurologist turned teacher and author, suggests that students should be able to answer the question, "Why are we learning about this?" at any time (Willis, 2007). Of course, it is also important that the answer be personally relevant to them. In fact, some studies suggest that students believing, or not believing, that what they are learning will be useful in their lives is the most important indicator as to whether or not they will respond positively to the lesson (Jensen, 2000, p. 109).

Although how to make the lesson relevant is dependent on the content of the lesson, here are some ideas:

- Remind students how the lesson might connect to their goals (see the motivation chapter).

- Refer to "The Helping in the Future Lesson Plan" (if that had been taught; see page 27) and related posters on the wall created by students.

- Provide additional explicit suggestions on how students will be able to *transfer* what they will learn today to what they will learn in other classes and aspects of their lives. This is often challenging for students to identify on their own (Sousa, 2006, p. 138). Teachers can provide assignments to help students make those connections. Figure 8.1 (page 118) is an example made for an English class.

- Having students create a K-W-L chart (What I Know, What I Want To Know, and What I Have Learned), and explain that we tend to learn best when we can connect new information to what we already know.

Figure 8.1. Transfer Assignment Example

Name: _____

Date: _____

Homework Slip

English 9

Your "homework" is to use the reading strategy of *connecting* in one of your other classes today.

Directions:

Pick a piece of text you read in another class and connect it to something else. How does it relate to another piece of text? Television? The world? Your life? Something else?

Class:_____

What is this text about?

This connects to:

Explain how the two things connect:

Developed by Lara Hoekstra and reprinted with her permission.

- Pointing out that our brain naturally seeks patterns, and we are taking advantage of that tendency when we organize new information into categories (such as when we use data sets like the one in the motivation chapter).

- Reminding students about the benefits of "grit," "growth mindset," and "problems as opportunities," which they learned in previous lesson plans—assuming they had been done—where a lesson's applicability might not be clearcut or some students are having difficulty making those connections. This could be a time to tell students of a study released in 2010 that indicated having the qualities of "patience, discipline, manners, perseverance" could mean learners could earn in their lifetime $320,000 more than their counterparts without those qualities (Leonhardt, 2010).

- Telling students, as a last resort, it will be on a test (either one in class or a standardized one) might be characterized as helping to make a lesson personally relevant. Having students think that is the only reason they should learn something new is probably not the message we want to send, but I know few teachers who have not resorted to saying that on occasion (including me!).

Written and Verbal Instructions

Writing down short instructions for students on a whiteboard or overhead/document camera, as well as explaining them verbally, is another aspect of "strategic introductions." These kinds of "multiple stimulations" can enhance memory (Willis, 2006, p. 4). Even when students still forget what to do, teachers can then just point to the instructions instead of repeating them again…and again…and again.

However, if there will be several steps that students will need to do, it might be better to keep them hidden and uncover them one at a time. Doing so can avoid confusion and students trying to jump ahead without completing the necessary initial steps.

Modeling

One of the biggest lessons teachers learn is the importance of modeling for students before they are expected to do a particular assignment. Teacher modeling seems to make a huge difference, and is recommended by many researchers, including Robert Marzano ("Holt McDougal Literature," 2010). No matter the subject, providing examples, including explicitly modeling the thinking process the teacher is using, will go a long way toward ensuring student success.

If you have a document camera in your room, however, nothing beats having students bring up examples of their work or just having the teacher grab the sheets and show them to the class during the lesson itself. By using that kind of modeling, you help other students see how to do it, take advantage of the fact that peer modeling can be more effective with young people (Berten, 2008), and provide unexpected recognition of good work, which is the kind of reward that does not reduce intrinsic motivation (Pink, 2009, p. 204).

Activate Prior Knowledge

We can help students make what they are learning more "meaning-ful" by helping them connect it to something they already know (Wolfe, 2001, p. 104). This can be done by the kinds of questions listed under "Novelty" (see page 116) or by the activities listed under "Relevance" (see page 117). Reminding students of how what they are going to learn, or are learning, on that day relates to what they have previously learned can also help them make that connection.

Translating

Whether it's during the introductory phase of a lesson, or at other times, asking students to "translate" important concepts into their own words can be a useful exercise. It could be as simple as asking them to tell their neighbor what the instructions are for the lesson that the teacher just provided. Or doing the same thing with a passage the class read, or certain important vocabulary words.

Movement

When we move, our blood recirculates and can result is as much as an additional 15% more blood in the brain (Sousa, 2006, p. 34). In addition, studies with adolescents indicate that nearly 75% of those studied were better learners when movement was incorporated into their classroom environment (Jensen, 2000, p. 110).

Creating opportunities for students to move—at least a bit—during lessons can help a lesson be successful. Students could move to be with a partner for a quick "think-pair-share" activity, or go to a small group to work on a project for a longer time. Students could have prearranged partners and locations that are the same for a week or two to facilitate movement.

Choices

William Glasser identified power and freedom as two of the basic needs that all humans have (Glasser, 1986, p. 25). Providing students with options to choose from is one way to help students experience both. Having some authority over how one learns something new also improves the ability to remember it ("How Taking an Active Role," 2010) and increases students levels of interest (Sparks, 2010). Most dictionaries define power as "the ability to act" and having the freedom to choose (act) can enhance students' sense of control and help them develop self-confidence (Zadina, 2008, p. 51). These choices could include being:

- Asked on occasion for their partner preferences.

- Allowed to choose which reading strategies (visualization, making a connection, evaluating, asking a question, summarizing) they would demonstrate on a piece of text.

- Invited to choose where they would like to sit during small group sessions.

- Given two or more options of writing prompts to respond to.

These suggestions, however, do have one caveat. Sheena Iyengar (2010) has researched the idea of choice across cultures and found that some students in some cultures, particularly Asian ones, can perform *worse* when given the opportunity to make choices. Consequently, even though providing options to most students in U.S. classrooms can improve academic performance, teachers should be conscious of exceptions to the rule (as well as to any other educational or school "rule").

Minimize Lecture & Maximize Cooperative Learning

Research is cited in Question 1 on motivating students that finds lecturing is one of the less-effective teaching methods available. Multiple studies have found that cooperative learning is often a more valuable alternative. One of many reasons for cooperative learning's success is that it helps students achieve another of Glasser's basic human needs—to belong and connect (Glasser, 1988, p. 25).

Question 11 on cooperative learning shares more ideas on how this learning method can be incorporated in a lesson. As discussed in that chapter, studies show that smaller, rather than larger, groups work best, with three or four students being the maximum. I personally prefer sticking with pairs for most of a school year, and possibly moving it to three near the last quarter after six months of student experience with the process.

Wait Time

The average time between a teacher posing a question and a student giving the answer in a typical classroom is approximately one second. With this tiny amount of time, many students tend to give short and simple answers or no answers at all. Multiple studies show that the quality and quantity of student responses increases when the wait time (also called think time) is increased to between three and seven seconds ("Wait Time," n.d.). In addition, those same studies show that after teachers begin to implement this methodology, their *questions,* too, become much better at promoting higher-order thinking (Stahl, n.d.).

One way to implement this kind of "think time" is to use the process of "Think-Pair-Share" by announcing:

> I'm going to ask a question, but I don't anyone to answer it right away. I want you think about it for a few seconds without saying anything.

Teacher poses the question and says:

> Now, I want you to share your answer with a person near you.

Next, the teacher can begin calling on people to share their responses with the entire class. It is also possible to incorporate another step into the process and make it a "Think-Write-Pair-Share."

Another option is to say:

> I'm going to ask a question, but I don't anyone to respond. I want you to take a few seconds to think about it, and then I'll call on people.

After the teacher, and students, get into the habit of handling questions and answers this way, this kind introduction might not be necessary—students will just know they will have a few seconds to prepare their response to teacher questions, and that you might call on any one (or two or three) of them. By not calling out the name of an individual student prior to asking the question, any student knows he/she might be asked to respond. By using this process, you can, in effect, institute a "no hands policy" (or a quasi "no hands" policy) where all students think they need to be prepared at all times. An additional way to encourage student response and reduce their fear of being "ambushed" is by incorporating a suggestion made by a former teacher blogger who wrote under the pen name California Teacher Guy. He suggests putting up two signs next to each other on the classroom wall. One says "I Don't Know" with a line drawn through it. The other says "I'm Not Sure, But I Think That...."

By combining these factors, teachers have the potential to create a classroom atmosphere of "relaxed alertness" that researchers Renate and Geoffrey Caine call the "optimum emotional climate for learning" (Caine, 2009, p. 21).

Visuals

Many studies have shown that memory and learning can be enhanced by using photos and other imagery (Wolfe, 2001, p. 154). Our eyes contain

70% of our body's sensory receptors (Wolfe, 2001, p. 152), and with written, verbal, and imagery input our brain is able to create multiple connections (Willis, 2006, p. 4).

Photos can be used to increase vocabulary comprehension by connecting them with new words. They can be used to promote higher-order thinking by having students generate questions about them and hypotheses about what they represent. Students can also be asked to apply standard reading strategies (making a connection, prediction, etc.) to a photo. Or, as mentioned in the "Strategic Introductions" section (see page 116), an attention-grabbing picture can be a useful lesson introduction.

Many more ideas on how to use photos in the classroom can be found at http://larryferlazzo.edublogs.org/2010/06/27/the-best-ways-to-use-photos-in-lessons/.

Short video clips (some researchers recommend showing video clips for no longer than ten minutes at a time; see Zhu, 2010) can be used in similar ways. Be sure that the assignment is clear prior to showing the video.

Explicit Pattern Seeking

The brain is designed to see the world through a lens of seeking and generating patterns; it is how we make sense of the world and create meaning. Students are always creating meanings this way, and it is sometimes similar to the old community organizing adage that "all communities are already organized, they just tend to be organized in the wrong way." A challenge to teachers is to guide this natural impulse into the areas of "...problem solving and critical thinking. Although we choose much of what students are to learn, the ideal process is to present the information in a way that allows brains to extract patterns, rather than attempt to impose them" (Caine & Caine, 1994, p. 89).

When we provide students pattern-seeking opportunities, they can increase brain cell activity and enhance memory and learning (Willis, 2006, p. 15).

The section on incorporating higher-orders of thinking in lessons (see page 131) offers detailed and practical suggestions on using this strategy. You can also find examples of the pattern-seeking methods of concept attainment and inductive learning (through using data sets) in lessons located in Question 1.

Using graphic organizers is another common and effective tool that is recommended by Robert Marzano and others to facilitate pattern-seeking (Marzano, 2001, p. 75). A K-W-L chart (What Do I Know? What Do I Want to Know? What Have I Learned?) may be the most familiar example of a graphic organizer. Many other outlines can be found at http://larryferlazzo.edublogs.org/2009/02/09/not-the-best-but-a-list-of-mindmapping-flow-chart-tools-graphic-organizers/.

Fun

William Glasser (1988) identifies having fun as one of the five basic psychological needs that all humans need. Certainly, at its best, learning something new that is personally relevant to the learner and gained through an engaging lesson plan can be fun.

In addition, teachers can try to be more explicit in using other kinds of "fun" in lessons. A sense of humor that results in student laughter (or even smiles or groans) can have many positive effects on the learning process, including generating more oxygen for the brain and releasing endorphins in the blood that enhances attention (Sousa, 2009, p. 63).

Games can also be a source of fun and learning. Question 13 on incorporating games goes into more detail about how to use them. They can be good tools for review, and can function as a quick three-minute break or transition time. For example, putting a lesson-related "sentence scramble" (words from a sentence that are out of order) on the whiteboard, giving students the option to work in pairs or on their own to "unscramble" it, and offering a few points of extra credit or some other minor reward to the first seven people who get it right can take generate a big positive gain in the classroom climate at very little "cost."

Just "framing" a lesson as "fun" has been found to result in increased student achievement (DiSalvo, 2010, August 24) and enhances student insight and creativity (Carey, 2010). Introducing clozes (fill-in-the-blank passages) and sequencing activities as puzzles are examples of this kind of effective reframing.

Feedback

Question 5, the problems as opportunities chapter, highlights the importance of giving students feedback for their effort and not their intelligence. In addition, it has been found that if students are expecting to receive "rapid" feedback—a teacher's verbal or written response shortly after the work or test is completed—the quality of student work increases. Researchers think this may be because people are more likely to want to avoid feeling disappointed with a less-than-positive reaction. If the feedback is going to happen later, the concern about disappointment does not seem as immediate (DiSalvo, 2010, March 11).

Expecting immediate written feedback from most teachers most of the time is problematic, especially in secondary schools with large student populations. But as long as teachers are constantly circulating during class time when students are working, there is no reason why this kind of immediate verbal feedback can't take place. In addition, teachers can easily create a simple rubric to complete when individual students or small groups are making presentations. This completed sheet can be given to the group during the same day.

Formative Assessment

Formative assessments are ongoing practices that help both the teacher and student evaluate and reflect on how they are both doing, and what changes either or both might need to make to become a more effective teacher and learner. These can include strategies like asking students to "show with their thumbs" if a concept is clear; carefully circulating and observing students; having them explain an idea to each other in pairs; and completing cloze (fill-in-the-blank) and reading fluency assessments described in Question 6. The ideas in the "Reflection, Review, & Summarization" section below and in Question 7 also fall into this category.

Formative assessments are often contrasted with *summative* assessments. Summative assessments are the midterm and final exams, benchmarks, and state tests that we give. They are designed to, at least theoretically, tell us what a student has learned and what the student hasn't learned and tend to be used to assess a grade or ranking.

Formative assessments are generally considered more useful to teachers. To quote Robert Marzano (2007, p. 13) formative assessments "might be one of the more powerful weapons in a teacher's arsenal."

More information on formative assessment can be found at http://larryferlazzo.edublogs.org/2010/08/22/the-best-resources-for-learning-about-formative-assessment/.

Reflection, Review, & Summarization

Question 9, regarding how to use "leftover" class time, describes the research, reasoning behind, and processes for using reflection, active review, and summarization. The most important thing that teachers should remember about implementing any one of the three is that the students need to take the primary responsibility of doing it. As Patricia Wolfe writes (2001, p. 187):

> **Remember that the person doing the work is the one growing the dendrites.**

Dendrites are the parts of the brain that grow as we learn new things (Willis, 2006, p. 1). Teachers might want to tape this sentence to their desks!

How Can You Best Use a Few Minutes of "Leftover" Time in Class?*

I've just completed my lesson plan for the day, and there are five more minutes before the bell rings. There's not enough time to start the next day's lesson, and I don't really want to give students five minutes of free time—class time is too valuable; if I do it once I'm concerned they'll want it often, and I just know if I give it to them today my principal will pick that time to come in to observe your class. Plus, five minutes is long enough for kids to get into trouble. What do should I do?

There are many options for this kind of situation, including Review, Summarize, Relate, Reflect, Intellectually Challenge, Technologically Engage, and Read.

Review

Research shows that you have to see a new word more than ten times (and in different contexts) to really learn it (Schmitt, n.d.). Studies differ on the number of times we need to review a new piece of information before

---

* Portions of this chapter originally appeared in *Teacher Magazine* (2009).

it's ours, but it's more than a few. Review is one good use of those extra minutes. It could be done in a game format with students divided into teams that have to answer questions spoken or written on the whiteboard. Students could break into pairs and quiz each other. To add a little intrigue, Student A could give the answer and Student B has to supply the question, Jeopardy style.

Summarize

Rick Wormeli wrote an excellent book titled *Summarization in Any Subject: 50 Techniques to Improve Student Learning* (2004). In it, he provides a wealth of research, including from Robert Marzano, which demonstrates the importance of having students summarize what they have been studying (Wormeli, 2004, p. 2). The book also includes many practical summarization activities.

Typical end-of-class exercises include students writing:

- What are three things you learned?

- What is the most interesting thing you've learned?

- Imagine a simile or a metaphor about what we learned today.

Students write them down on a sheet, and then share with a partner before the teacher calls on some students to share with the entire class.

Relate

In an exhaustive review of 4,000 studies and articles in 2006, the Cooperative Learning Institute found that "over three-fourth's of the variation in academic achievement was explained by the quality of interpersonal relationships." The Institute wrote "a teacher's secret strategy for increasing student achievement may be building more positive relationships among students" (Johnson, Johnson, & Roseth, 2006, p. 3). Teachers could take advantage of any extra few minutes by structuring the time to help students learn more about each other and strengthen their relationships. Students could ask each other a series of questions about their preferences, goals, families, etc., with the goal of everybody having these conversations with everyone else.

Reflect

When philosopher Hannah Arendt observed the trial of Adolf Eichmann, the architect of the Holocaust, she wrote that she had expected to see a monster. Instead, she was shocked to see a man who was mechanical, bureaucratic, and thoughtless. Might evil, she wondered, often be the result of the absence of thought and reflection? (Arendt, 2006, p. 252) Without developing the capacity to reflect, we will not necessarily turn into war criminals like Eichmann, but we can become mechanical and live our life by a formula.

Because of this, it is important to regularly reinforce the value of reflection with our students. It's not something that comes naturally to most people, and certainly not to children. Teachers can help students to reflect by asking them to respond in writing to questions like:

- What, if anything, would you like to change about yourself and what is one thing you can do tomorrow to start?

- Describe one moment in your life when you felt you learned something important (practically no student of mine has ever written about something that happened in school).

- What do you do well, and what helps you be successful in doing it?

Teachers can also use this time as an opportunity to learn about what is going on in student's lives. This information can be used to initiate conversations to help strengthen teacher/student relationships and to help construct lessons that students might see as more relevant (see Question 1: How Do You Motivate Students?). Asking "What is the best thing that has happened to you this week and why is it such a good thing?"; "How are things going in your other classes?"; or a simple "How are things at home?" are some questions that could be used.

Reflective questions, of course, can also directly relate to what happened in the classroom that day. Some questions suggested by Project Zero, a Harvard program that studies multiple intelligences ("Project Zero," 2010) include:

- How does today's learning connect to what you already knew?

- How did it extend your thinking further?

- What questions do you still have?

Questions can also relate to the class in general, including ones like:

- Think of one thing you have learned this year in class that you can apply in another class or another part of your life. What is it, and how can you apply it?

- What is your favorite activity in this class? Why?

- What is your least favorite activity in this class? Why?

Robert Marzano (2001, p. 57) calls reflection "the final step in a comprehensive approach to actively processing information." One of the questions he recommends asking students is to share how well they think they did in class and what they believe they could have done better.

Former Harvard professor Tal Ben-Sahar cites research from MIT that appears to confirm Marzano's perspective:

> What the results suggest is that while there certainly is some record of your experience as it is occurring…the actual learning—when you try to figure out: "What was important? What should I keep and throw away?"—that happens after the fact, during periods of quiet wakeful introspection. ("Can Stillness and Reflection," 2010).

A study by Neville Hatton and David Smith (1995) also suggests that sharing with others enhances self-reflection. After students respond in writing to a question or two, they could quickly talk about their responses with a partner.

Intellectually Challenge

Teachers can share "lateral-thinking puzzles"—a term coined by Edward de Bono to describe indirect approaches to problem solving. These are very short mysteries that require students to think outside the box. A quick search on Google will uncover many examples that you can use in your classroom. Here is a well-known example of one of these puzzles:

> Five pieces of coal, a carrot, and a scarf are lying on the lawn. Nobody put them on the lawn but there is a perfectly logical reason why they should be there. What is it?
>
> They were used by children who made a snowman. The snow has now melted. ("Lateral Solution," n.d.)

Challenging students to solve "sentence scrambles"—words from one sentence that are written out of order and need to be rewritten correctly—can be another activity that fits in this category. Having students work on one or two scrambles that have been written on the board, and offering some small prize to the first several pairs that solve them correctly could add a little more fun to the exercise.

Technologically Engage

If you happen to be in the computer lab (or if you are teaching a class where all students have Web access), many teachers have created websites that have links to engaging and reinforcing learning activities. Students can be easily directed to specific sites or given freedom to roam links on a page you've created or previewed.

Learning games are always useful, and there are many teacher-reviewed lists on the Internet (see, e.g., http://larryferlazzo.edublogs.org/2010/08/28/a-collection-of-the-best-lists-on-games/). Better yet, students can easily create their own learning games (http://larryferlazzo.edublogs.org/2008/04/21/the-best-websites-for-creating-online-learning-games/).

Read

Many schools have students choose their own high-interest books for pleasure reading. If you teach in a school with that practice, students can always read their own books for a few minutes. Teachers can also have copies of engaging and lesson-related magazines available.

In addition, teachers reading aloud an engaging piece of literature can grab students' attention—at any age.

No matter what you think of the Boy Scouts, their motto, "Be Prepared" is a good one. Having these seven options in your "back pocket" is one way to act on that scout advice.

The Importance of Good Endings

The title of this chapter is somewhat of a misnomer. The reason why "leftover" is in quotation marks is because no such thing really exists in the classroom. In many ways, the last few minutes of a class period might be the most important class time of all.

As mentioned previously, in a public lecture in 2010, Nobel Prize winner Daniel Kahneman (2010) elaborates on this topic. He begins by telling the story of a friend who listened to twenty minutes of wonderful classical music that ended with a terrible screech on the recording. His friend said that the ending ruined it all for him.

The answer to Question 7 described how Kahneman (2010) uses that story to frame how he says we think—we have an "experiencing self" and a "remembering self." The experiencing self is when a doctor asks if it hurts when he touches a certain place, while the remembering self responds to a question about how you have been feeling lately.

The remembering self is key because we use those memories, and the stories we turn them into, when we make future decisions.

We certainly want the "experiencing selves" of our students to feel like they've had a good learning experience in class, and can work hard at making that happen through all the resources at our disposal. But whether or not that happens all the time—not all lessons hit homeruns, and there are just days when students (and teachers) are not feeling great—we can work hard in the final minutes to ensure that their "remembering selves" definitely have a good story about the day.

How Can You Help Students Develop Higher-Order Thinking Skills?

I want to incorporate more higher-order thinking skills in my class, but I'm not exactly sure what "higher-order thinking skills" means and how to do it. Yes, I've heard of Bloom's Taxonomy and, in fact, have a version hanging on my classroom wall. But what do I do with it?!?

First, let's take a minute to clarify what "higher-order thinking skills" (or HOTS) actually means. It is commonly thought of as the ability to apply knowledge and concepts to problem solving and critical thinking. In effect, it is the construction of new knowledge ("Higher-Order Thinking," 2004). By developing these higher-order thinking skills, students are more likely to be able to apply what they know to new situations.

"Lower-order thinking skills" (or LOTS), on the other hand, are more likely to focus on recalling and reproducing existing knowledge, and on following rules ("Higher-Order Thinking," 2004).

> **We are using LOTS when we use our keys to start the car. We are using HOTs when we have to figure out what to do when it doesn't start or breaks down when we're driving.**

The differences between the HOTS and LOTS were brought into focus by the development of Bloom's Taxonomy, developed by a group led by Benjamin Bloom in 1956. It was an effort to classify thinking into six levels of increasing complexity. In 2001, another group unveiled a Revised Bloom's Taxonomy that made several modifications, including changing the names of the levels into verbs (you can read more about the Taxonomy's history at http://projects.coe.uga.edu/epltt/index.php?title=Bloom's_Taxonomy).

This chapter uses the Revised Taxonomy (Figure 10.1). Although different presentations of the Taxonomy abound in print and on the Web, this particular figure has been modified from a chart published by one of the creators of the Revised Bloom's Taxonomy, David R. Krathwohl (2002, p. 215) because, among other things, it is designed to be more accessible to students. However, because the differences between the original and revised versions are not particularly significant in how either teachers or students would apply them, the ideas listed here are applicable no matter which version you use.

Although Bloom originally thought that students had to "move up the ladder" systematically, more recent studies show that all students can benefit from higher-order-thinking-skill development and, in fact, some previously "low-achieving" students can even make greater net academic gains than "higher-achieving" ones (http://www.jstor.org/pss/1466891). Of course, in this instruction, as with all others, some students might require more scaffolding and support than others.

The Revised Bloom's Taxonomy provides more recognition of this fact by "blurring" the lines between the levels. It recognizes that many similar skills can be used in all six levels (Krathwohl, 2002, p. 215).

The Taxonomy does not say that the lower levels of thinking that require recall and understanding of facts are "bad." Its classification system just reminds us that helping our students learn the facts as we know them today is just one element of the purpose of education. We must also help students develop higher-thinking skills so they can be prepared to learn and understand what new discoveries and our changing world might say and change about what we think we know now. Some also wonder how much emphasis should be spent on recalling information in the age of immediate Internet access, as well (Frean, 2008).

The Taxonomy is best viewed by teachers through the lens of an old community organizing adage: "It's a compass, not a map." Looking at it this way provides educators the flexibility they need to most effectively teach our diverse students across grade levels.

This chapter shares some immediate steps that teachers can take to help their students develop higher-level thinking skills, as well as actions to "set the stage." A lesson plan is also included.

Figure 10.1. Revised Bloom's Taxonomy (from Lowest to Highest, with Examples of Verbs for Objectives)

1. Remember—recalling the facts
   - Naming
   - Recalling
   - Reciting
   - Identifying

2. Understand—comprehension of meaning
   - Explaining
   - Summarizing
   - Paraphrasing
   - Restating

3. Apply—using a specific process when called for
   - Implementing
   - Experimenting
   - Practicing
   - Using

4. Analyze—breaking down into parts and identifying how they relate to each other
   - Categorizing
   - Classifying
   - Comparing
   - Organizing
   - Connecting

5. Evaluate—making a judgment and giving reasons
   - Deciding
   - Recommending
   - Choosing
   - Defending

6. Create—connecting parts into a new pattern or making something new
   - Creating
   - Combining
   - Constructing
   - Originating
   - Inventing

Adapted from Krathwohl, D. (2002, p. 215; available at http://www.unco.edu/cetl/sir/stating_outcome/documents/Krathwohl.pdf).

Immediate Steps

Helping Students Develop Metacognition

Many of the topics covered in this book—students making goals, looking at how the brain works, encouraging a growth mindset, reflecting—relate to the idea of metacognition. As mentioned in earlier chapters, metacognition is the process of looking at one's own thinking process. Without it, we might continue to make the same mistakes over and over again, miss opportunities to see patterns or effective shortcuts, and be unable to systematically apply our strengths and compensate for our weaknesses. Metacognition is continually asking certain questions of ourselves: Based on what we know about our strengths, interests, and weaknesses, and what we have learned and experienced in the past, what is the best way for us to approach this particular situation? For example, I may know it works best for me to write an outline before I write an essay, or that when I read I remember best by highlighting three or four words per paragraph, or that biology is harder for me so I should set aside more time to read the textbook.

Metacognition might be less necessary in the lowest level of Bloom's—Remember—because its focus is on recalling basic facts with little interpretation. However, the remaining five levels require students to explore patterns, develop connections, and make judgments of increasing complexity. These actions, if done wisely, all require the student to be able to answer the question "Why?" Being able to answer that question generally means the student must be able to explain his/her thinking process.

By teaching metacognition explicitly, and helping students become conscious of its importance and how to use it strategically, the hope is that metacognition will eventually lead to automaticity. This means that students would exercise metacognition without having to consciously think about it (Tileston, 2004).

Two ways to immediately implement the idea of teaching metacognition is by asking students questions related to higher-order thinking skills and by teachers modeling their own thinking processes.

Asking Questions

Many of the previous chapters reviewed various opportunities teachers might have to ask questions promoting metacognition, including ones related to motivation, goal setting, and reflection. Asking students these kinds questions—What made you decide to start the essay with that opening? How were you able to maintain such good self-control this class period? What clues did you use to lead you to writing this word into the blank?—can promote their "thinking about their thinking."

Project Zero, a research and development group at the Harvard Graduate School of Education, encourages teachers to keep a simple "thinking routine" composed of two questions in mind: "What's going on here?" and "What do you see that makes you say so?" This is one example of how this thinking routine might work:

...[A] teacher might show students a satellite photograph of a hurricane without identifying it, and ask, "What's going on here?" One student says, "That's a storm over Florida." The teacher asks, "What do you see that makes you say so?" The student points out the distinctive profile of Florida, visible through the clouds. Another student says, "It's a hurricane." The teacher: "What do you see that makes you say hurricane?" The student mentions the size of the cloud structure and its spiral formation. Another student adds by identifying the eye in the middle. (Perkins, 2003, para. 7)

The idea behind a "thinking routine" is that it can be used regularly across the curriculum to develop higher-order thinking skills.

Teachers Modeling Their Thinking Process

"Think Alouds" are one name to call moments when teachers model their thinking process. Pebble Creek Labs, which trains teachers in instructional strategies, describes them as making "the unseen seen, the unconscious conscious" ("Think Aloud Strategy Summary," n.d.).

Here is an example of a Think Aloud using an excerpt from Luis Rodriguez' popular book, *Always Running* (2005). While reading the excerpt, the teacher would interject the comments in bold.

Read Aloud: Rodriguez Excerpt

 We never stopped crossing borders. **[This makes me remember when I had to cross the border to visit Mexico.]** The Río Grande (or Río Bravo, which is what the Mexicans call it, giving the name a power "Río Grande" just doesn't have) was only the first of countless barriers set in our path.

We kept jumping hurdles, kept breaking from the constraints, kept evading the border guards of every new trek. It was a metaphor to fill our lives—that river, that first crossing, the mother of all crossings. The L.A. River, for example, became a new barrier, keeping the Mexicans in their neighborhoods over on the vast east side of the city for years, except for forays downtown. Schools provided other restrictions: Don't speak Spanish, don't be Mexican—you don't belong. **[This reminds me of so many other people in our country's history who faced prejudice. What makes people so afraid of newcomers?]** Railroad tracks divided us from communities where white people lived, such as South Gate and Lynwood across from Watts. **[I wonder what barriers people might find in our own community? Even in our own school?]**

We were invisible people in a city which thrived on glitter, big screens, and big names, but this glamour contained none of our names, none of our faces. The refrain "this is not your country" echoed for a lifetime. **[When facing such huge obstacles, I wonder what would make it worth continuing to fight?]** (Rodriguez, 2005, p. 19).

Regularly modeling these kinds of thinking processes will be useful at all times. However, they will be most helpful after explicitly teaching the elements of Bloom's Taxonomy and providing students times to practice them.

Setting the Stage

Graphic Organizers

Graphic organizers (see Question 8 regarding how to ensure a lesson is successful) can help a student organize his/her own thinking. Though graphic organizers can be used simply to record facts, they can also be designed to stimulate higher-order thinking. In fact, Robert Marzano cites research that using graphic organizers and other "nonlinguistic representations" actually "stimulates and increases activity in the brain" (Marzano, 2001, p. 73). Although there are many graphic organizer options, here are three in particular that can develop higher-order thinking skills:

- The familiar Venn Diagram to help compare and contrast. This can be expanded from two to three or four circles to provide an increasing challenge.

- K-W-L charts (What Do I Know? What Do I Want to Know? What Have I Learned) help make connections. These can be particularly helpful to developing higher-order thinking skills if each item in each column is explicitly connected. For example, if a student is doing a K-W-L chart about New York City, the student could put down that he knows there was a terrorist attack there on 9/11 in the "Know" column; right next to that item in the "Want to Know" column he could write, "Why was the World Trade Center chosen for the attack?" Then later he can write down the answer or answers to his question under the "Learned" section. Using a graphic organizer in this way can lead to more higher-order thinking skills than the disconnected items that are often listed in K-W-L charts. When introducing K-W-L charts, it is a good idea to explain to students another reason why they are useful: because we learn better when we can connect new information and concepts to something we already know.

- Kelly Young at Pebble Creek Labs encourages teachers to use clozes (also known as "gap-fill" exercises) along with a simple graphic organizer. Figure 10.2 is a cloze for Beginning English Language Learners; however, clozes can be created using text at any level of difficulty. The graphic organizer in Figure 10.3 (page 138) challenges readers of the cloze to articulate *why* they wrote the word they chose for the blank—Were there clue words? Was there something about the tense of the verb in the sentence? A similar graphic organizer can be used for many different class projects.

- In addition to these three graphic organizer options (and many more you can find at http://larryferlazzo.edublogs. org/2009/02/09/not-the-best-but-a-list-of-mindmapping-flow-chart-tools-graphic-organizers/), after students have seen a few different graphic organizers and are more familiar with the Revised Bloom's Taxonomy, you can challenge students to create their own for different lessons and explain why they designed them the way they did.

Figure 10.2. Jobs Cloze

People need to earn money to pay for food to eat and a place to live. People work at (1) _____ to get money. Most adults work at jobs. The (2) _____ you get to work at a job is called a wage or a salary.

If you work at the same kind of job for a long time then you have a career. Most people have more than one (3) _____ during their lives.

People who graduate from high school make more money than people who do not (4) _____ from high school. You can make even more (5) _____ if you go to college.

It is important to work at a job to make money. It is also (6) _____ to work at a job you like. Some people find a job they like to do. Some people do not like to work for somebody else. (7) _____ start their own business.

Some people work for the government by becoming a teacher, a police officer, or a firefighter. There are many different types of government (8) _____. People can also join the military.

As you can see, there are many different kinds of jobs. Students have a few years before they decide which one kind of job they want to do in their lives.

Figure 10.3. Cloze Answer Sheet

Please write down the word you put in each blank and explain why you chose that word. For example, did another word in the cloze give you a clue?

WORD YOU CHOSE	YOUR REASON
1.	
2.	
3.	
4.	
5.	
6.	
7.	
8.	

Use a Bloom's Taxonomy Chart in Your Lesson Planning

Whether it's the one in Figure 10.1 (page 133), or any of the countless other versions you can find online (see http://larryferlazzo.edublogs.org/2009/05/25/the-best-resources-for-helping-teachers-use-blooms-taxonomy-in-the-classroom/), a Taxonomy chart is a useful guide and reminder to have around when you are planning lessons. It is not a strict checklist that has to be used to ensure that every single lesson utilizes every single HOTS level. Instead, it is a compass to use and reflect on which levels your lessons are tending to include.

It is, however, not too difficult to incorporate several levels into many lessons. For example, a lesson using the cloze in Figure 10.3, and using some of the suggestions from Pebble Creek Labs on how to effectively teach it (Cloze strategy summary, n.d.), could be looked at through the lens of the levels of the Revised Bloom's Taxonomy in these ways (note that these are not listed in the chronological order in which they would occur):

- ◆ *Remember*—After reading it with the class, the teacher could ask the students to share the main idea of the cloze. Students could also be asked to highlight words that are new to them. In addition, they could use the information in the cloze to add to a K-W-L chart on the topic.

- ◆ *Understand*—Students could draw a picture to visualize what they are reading. They could also try to determine the meanings of the new words they highlighted through a guided discussion on context clues, as well as looking up a few in the dictionary.

♦ *Apply*—Students can complete the procedure suggested by Pebble Creek Labs:

- Students should read the passage first.

- Think of several possibilities, then choose the best one.

- Fill in easy blanks first.

- Reread the whole passage at the end. (Cloze strategy summary, n.d.).

♦ *Analyze*—This level is part of the procedure: the thinking of several possibilities.

♦ *Evaluate*—Again, this is part of the procedure: choosing which is the best answer and then explaining their reasons in the graphic organizer.

♦ *Create*—Students could take a passage of their choice and create their own cloze (placing blanks strategically so that there are identifiable clues) for their classmates to complete.

This lesson is an example of how the levels in the Revised Bloom's Taxonomy can flow into each other, yet still achieve the purpose of encouraging higher-order thinking skills.

Similar correlations with the Revised Bloom's Taxonomy can be made in most other lessons in this book, including in the examples of concept attainment and inductive learning in the Question 1 on student motivation.

Incorporating Inductive Learning

Teaching *inductively* is another method to develop higher-level thinking skills. As mentioned in Question 8, teaching inductively uses the brain's natural inclination to seek and generate patterns to guide it toward the levels of analyzing, evaluating, and creating. Typically, students are provided a series of examples that they can categorize and use to create concepts or rules. Question 1 on student motivation has examples of how this can be used to help students refine their writing through the inductive method of "concept attainment." That same chapter provides a lesson plan on students using a "data set" compiled of student-generated writing to help them identify how what they are learning today might help them in the future.

Teaching *deductively*, on the other hand, generally means providing the concepts or rules to students first and then having them practice applying those same concepts or rules.

Multiple studies have found inductive teaching to be effective (Joyce & Weil, 2009, p. 88). In one, fourth graders used to the inductive model to:

> ...explore the techniques used by published authors to accomplish tasks such as announcing the main idea clearly, introducing characters, establishing setting, and describing actions. The students, having characterized several devices that authors use for accomplishing similar tasks, then experimented with those devices in their own writing....Their end-of-year scores for writing quality were higher than the en-of-year scores for eighth grade students the previous year! (Joyce & Calhoun, 1998, p. 178)

In addition to the data set found in Question 1, the student motivation chapter, another example can be found in Figure 10.4. This data set on San Francisco is designed for Early Intermediate English Language Learners, though, like clozes, they can be developed for any grade, subject, or language level student.

Any lesson using a data set can follow the model laid out in the student motivation chapter lesson plan (see page 27). Here they are restated in the context of the Revised Bloom's Taxonomy and using the steps as described (in a modified form) by Kelly Young of Pebble Creek Labs, who is a national leader in training teachers to use inductive learning (Inductive model summary, n.d.):

- *Remember*—Examining the Data Set: Students read the examples, either in pairs or on their own, identifying the main idea in each example.

- *Understand*—Continue to examine the data set, perhaps by summarizing some and demonstrating other reading strategies (visualizing, making a connect, etc.) in others.

- *Apply*—Concept Formation: Classify the examples into teacher- or student-identified categories.

- *Analyze & Evaluate*—Interpret the Data: Identify the attributes (the key common characteristics) within each category.

- *Create*—Students find examples of new information to add to their categories or use existing examples to "mimic write" their own. They turn their categories into paragraphs and their paragraphs into essays. They create completely new data sets.

Once again, it is clear that the Revised Bloom's Taxonomy levels are not individual "silos." In fact, their flexibility reflects the dynamism of the learning process.

Figure 10.4. San Francisco Data Set

Categories: History; Weather; Interesting Places to See

1. In 1775, Juan Manuel de Ayala was the first person from Europe to go to San Francisco.

2. It does not snow in San Francisco.

3. San Francisco grew from 500 people to 25,000 people in 1849 after gold was discovered in California.

4. Sixty-seven people died in San Francisco after an earthquake in 1989.

5. There was a prison on Alcatraz Island in the San Francisco Bay.

6. San Francisco is famous for its cable cars. Cable cars are like little buses.

7. Thirty thousand Chinese live in Chinatown in San Francisco.

8. Sea lions live on Fisherman's Wharf.

9. The water in San Francisco bay is very cold.

10. The Golden Gate Bridge goes over San Francisco Bay.

11. Coit Tower was built to honor firefighters.

12. There is fog in San Francisco on many days.

13. Half of San Francisco was destroyed by an earthquake and fire in 1906.

Cooperative Learning

Some cooperative learning models can be used effectively to develop students' higher-thinking skills. Question 11, on cooperative learning, explores their use in more detail.

Explicitly Teach the Revised (or Original) Bloom's Taxonomy

Teaching students what the Revised Bloom's Taxonomy is, how it can be used, and what advantages it provides them is an important step toward incorporating higher-order thinking skills in the classroom. The following lesson plan is one way to do just that.

Bloom's Taxonomy Lesson Plan*

Instructional Objectives

Students Will:

1. Learn about the Revised Bloom's Taxonomy.

2. Learn how to apply it in their lives and in the classroom.

Duration

Two 55-minute class periods

Common Core English Language Arts Standards

Reading:

1. Determine central ideas or themes of a text and analyze their development; summarize the key supporting details and ideas.

Writing:

1. Produce clear and coherent writing in which the development, organization, and style are appropriate to task, purpose, and audience.

Speaking & Listening:

1. Prepare for and participate effectively in a range of conversations and collaborations with diverse partners, building on others' ideas and expressing their own clearly and persuasively.

2. Adapt speech to a variety of contexts and communicative tasks, demonstrating command of formal English when indicated or appropriate.

Language:

1. Demonstrate command of the conventions of standard English grammar and usage when writing or speaking.

2. Demonstrate command of the conventions of standard English capitalization, punctuation, and spelling when writing.

Materials

1. Whiteboard or overhead projector/document camera

---

* Parts of this lesson have been adapted, with permission, from one developed by Kelly Young at Pebble Creek Labs http://pebblecreeklabs.com/.

2. Student copies of Revised Bloom's Taxonomy "questions stems" (http://www.robeson.k12.nc.us/1053209782552340/blank/browse.asp?A=383&BMDRN=2000&BCOB=0&C=87278 or search Internet for "Revised Bloom's question stems")

3. Student copies of Bloom's description Figure 10.1 (page 133)

4. Easel paper

5. Internet access and a computer projector (optional)

6. Student copies of "The Three Little Pigs" (Figure 10.5, page 147)

Procedure

First Day

1. Teacher says something like: "Everybody, take a minute and think of three things that you're good at—video games, basketball, cooking—and write them down. Try to think of three, but if you can't think of three, write as many as you can. If you can think of more, write down more." After a minute, the teacher tells students to share what they wrote with a partner, and then asks some students to share with the entire class.

2. The teacher asks some students how long it took for them to get good at doing what they say they can do well. Teacher explains that, unless you have superhuman powers, you don't get good at something immediately. It takes time.

3. The teacher continues to say something like: "For example, to become the great teacher I am [*this should be humorous*], I first remembered what my teachers were like—the good and the bad [*teacher writes "Remember" at the bottom of a pyramid on the overhead or whiteboard with an arrow next to "my teachers"*]. Then I began reading some stuff on teaching, talking to teachers, asking them questions. I began to understand a little bit more [*teacher writes "Understand" as the next level in a pyramid with an arrow next to "read books, talk to teachers"*]. Next I became a tutor and began to apply what I learned [*teacher writes "Apply" as the next level and connect it to "tutor" with an arrow*]. Then I analyzed how it went by going to school and comparing what I was doing with what I was being taught I was supposed to be doing, and I spent lot of time thinking about it [*teacher writes "Analyze" as the next level on the pyramid and uses an arrow to connect it to "compared to others"*]. Then I evaluated how I was doing and made changes [*teacher writes "Evaluate" on the next level and connects it to "decided what changes to make"*]. Finally, I was confident enough to create my own lessons and develop my own style [*teacher writes "Create" and connects it to "my own lessons and style"*].

4. The teacher says in a few minutes he is going to talk more about this pyramid. But right now he wants students to pick one of the items on the list they made and make a sheet like the one he just made. It does not have to have six levels, it can have fewer. He just wants students to try to think of the stages they went through to become good at something. They should try to think of as many stages as they can, and be prepared to explain it like the teacher did. The teacher gives them five minutes to create their own pyramid. Teacher circulates to identify pyramids that do a good job showing Revised Bloom's levels.

5. Students share their pyramids in partners.

6. Teacher explains that this pyramid represents something called "Bloom's Taxonomy" and writes that on the board or overhead. Teacher asks, "What do you think is the name of the person who created it?" (Again, adding a little humor). Teacher continues to explain that it's designed to demonstrate higher and higher levels of thinking. "Sometimes in school we teachers spend too much time testing you students on just what you remember."

7. Teacher grabs two or three good student pyramids to show on the document camera as examples. ("Would Johnny have gotten good at skateboarding if he just spent all his time watching others?" "Would Teresa gotten to be such a good reader if she just had her parents read to her all the time?") Teacher explains that teachers need to make sure that the class lessons challenge students at the higher levels, which is one reason he will often ask "Why?" after students give answers. It's also important for students to understand these levels so that they can challenge themselves by "thinking about their thinking." It's easier to stay thinking at the lower levels. We all know that good readers ask questions to themselves when they read. So, just by asking questions of ourselves at higher levels we force ourselves to dig deeper into what we are reading.

8. Teacher explains that one way the class will become more familiar with Bloom's Taxonomy is by practicing asking questions that relate to the different levels. The teacher gives students copies of "question stems" for *only the first two levels*. The sheets should also have a few words describing the level (Figure 10.1, page 133, could also be distributed). The materials section of the lesson plan indicates where the "stems" can be obtained online.

9. The teacher explains that he wants students to use these question stems ("What is…?" "Where is…? etc.) to write down two examples of questions at the "Remember" level that relate to whatever topic that the class has been studying. In addition, the teacher asks students to draw something simple that would illustrate the idea of "remember." The teacher asks stu-

dents to share what they wrote with a partner, and then asks a few students to share with the entire class. The teacher could have some students bring their drawing to the document camera.

10. Next, the teacher uses the same process with the "Understand" level ("How could you summarize…?" "Can you give an example of…? etc.).

11. The teacher then explains that each pair of students will receive an easel sheet of paper. Students should both contribute, and they should decide—of their four questions and four drawings—which is the best question and drawing for each level. They should reproduce them on the easel sheet and leave space for the remaining four levels that the class will do tomorrow. The teacher could show a very rough outline of what the poster could look like, but give a great deal of leeway to students for the actual design as long as there is space for all the levels.

12. Students work on their poster.

Second Day

1. Teacher spends a few minutes reviewing the taxonomy from the previous day using student pyramid examples and the posters.

2. Leaving a listing of Bloom's Taxonomy, perhaps a student's pyramid, on the overhead, the teacher says he is going to take a few more minutes to look at the taxonomy in a slightly different way. The teacher holds up a pen. Teacher asks, "What is this? What does it look like?" Then the teacher asks students to take a minute and think about the answer to his next question: "What level of Bloom's Taxonomy are these questions?" (*Remember*) Continuing to hold up the pen, the teacher can ask: "What is the pen used for? How else can it be used?" The teacher asks what level are these questions (*Understand*). Next, the teacher asks: "Now that we know what a pen is used for, how do you actually use it? Can someone come up and show me?" The teacher asks the class what level they are at now (*Apply*). Next, the teacher asks: "What are the different parts of the pen?" The teacher has a student take it apart (and leaves it apart). The teacher asks what level they are at (*Analyze*). Next the teacher asks: "How do we know a pen is the best tool for the job? What are the reasons why a pen would be better than another tool?" The teacher asks the class what level they are at now (*Evaluate*). Finally, the teacher asks: "Is there a way we can put this pen back together in a better way? Or can we invent a better pen?" The teacher asks the class what level they are at now (*Create*). [This analogy is adapted, with permission, from principals Scott Johnston and George Couros (2010).]

3. The teacher then distributes the question stems for the next two levels and repeats the same process from the previous day, having students work on their own to write two questions and a representative illustration, share them with a partner, and some share in class. The next two levels are *Apply* ("What would happen if...?" "How would you use...?") and *Analyze* ("What are the different parts of...? " "How would you classify...?"). Students would then work on these next two sections of their posters.

4. The teacher then distributes the question stems for the final two levels and repeats the same process for *Evaluate* ("Which is more important...?" "Which is better...?") and *Create* ("How would you design...?" "How could you change...?" "What could be a new way...?").

5. Students can share their posters with each other.

6. The teacher explains that students will periodically be asked to reflect and share how they used the higher levels of the taxonomy in their academic work.

7. The teacher ends the class with a "lighter" Bloom's Taxonomy activity—either showing a short online video that uses the movie *Pirates of the Caribbean* to illustrate Bloom's Taxonomy levels (http://www.youtube.com/watch?v=qjhKmhKjzsQ&feature=youtu.be) or challenging students to read *The Three Little Pigs* (Figure 10.5) and identify where the pigs used the different levels. (There are various answers to that question. The important thing is that students should be prepared to backup their answers with reasons. Students could work in pairs.)

Assessment

The teachers can create a rubric for the student Bloom's Taxonomy poster that is appropriate for their classroom situation.

Possible Extensions/Modifications

Students could write their own story that would demonstrate all the Bloom's Taxonomy levels, or work in groups to create one.

Ed Tech: Internet Scavenger Hunt

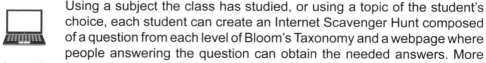

Using a subject the class has studied, or using a topic of the student's choice, each student can create an Internet Scavenger Hunt composed of a question from each level of Bloom's Taxonomy and a webpage where people answering the question can obtain the needed answers. More information on these scavenger hunts can be found at http://larryferlazzo.edublogs. org/2009/02/15/the-best-sources-for-internet-scavenger-hunts-webquests/.

Figure 10.5. The Three Little Pigs

Once upon a time, there were three pigs who left home to go see the world.

They had a great time that summer playing games and becoming friends with everyone they met. After a while, though, they saw that most people began to realize that the fall and winter were approaching, and people had less time to play with them. That made the pigs remember that winters could be pretty cold. They realized that if they didn't make homes for themselves, they would not have a place where they could stay warm and dry.

The three pigs, though, could not agree on what to do, so they each decided to build their own house.

The laziest pig said he would build a straw hut because it would be very easy to do. The others thought the straw would not hold up in the wintertime, and tried to convince him to build something stronger, but he would not listen. He built his straw house in a day.

The second pig decided he would build his house out of pieces of wood. He found a few, and spent two days quickly nailing them together.

The third pig, though, did not like either of the two houses. "You can't just throw together a house in a day or two. It takes time to make one strong enough to withstand the wind and snow, and to protect us from the big bad wolf!"

The third pig spent weeks building his house, brick by brick. The other two pigs tried to get him to play, and laughed at how much time he spent working on his home. But nothing could deter him from getting it finished.

One day, the pigs saw the tracks of the big bad wolf and they all ran to their homes.

The wolf chased them, and first went to the straw house. He said, "Come out, or I'll huff and puff and blow your house down!" The pig was afraid and refused. The wolf then blew with all his might and the straw house collapsed. The pig was lucky enough to escape to his brother's wood house.

The wolf followed him there and said again, "Come out, or I'll huff and puff and blow your house down!" The pigs refused. The wolf then blew with all his might and the flimsy wooden house collapsed. Luckily, the two pigs were able to escape to their brother's brick house.

The wolf followed them there, but was not able to blow the house down—it was built too well. Then, the wolf saw the chimney in the house and climbed to the roof. The wisest pig saw what he was going to do, and immediately lit the fire. The wolf slid down the chimney, but landed in the fire. He ran out of the house screaming and trying to put out the flames in his tail.

The wolf swore that he would never go down a chimney again.

After that terrible day, the two brothers whose houses were destroyed worked hard to build new brick homes. And anytime the wolf came to that neighborhood, he would see the three chimneys. They reminded him of the pain on that terrible day, and he never went near the three little pigs again.

And the three little pigs lived happily ever after.

Source: Adapted from Grimm's Fairy Tales.

Question 11

What Are the Best Ways to Incorporate Cooperative Learning in Your Lessons?

I know that having students work in groups is supposed to be good for learning, but the students just seem to get out of control every time I try it. It's gotten to the point that it is just not worth the trouble. How can I use cooperative learning in my classroom without it turning into a madhouse?

Cooperative learning—students thinking, talking, and working together instead of just sitting there and listening to the "sage on stage"—can be a potent instructional strategy if done well.

Robert Marzano (2007, p. 39) lists multiple studies that show cooperative learning can result in higher levels of student achievement. In addition to this result, Roger and David Johnson found after examining 122 studies that cooperative learning results in students feeling "more positive about school, subject areas, and teachers...more positive about each other...and are more effective interpersonally" (Johnson & Johnson, 1988).

This chapter shares suggestions for some "universal" guidelines to increase the chances of success with any cooperative learning activity. It also reviews several specific strategies to use in the classroom. A sample lesson plan is also included.

A Few "Universal" Guidelines

◆ Keep groups small. Research shows that the greatest individual academic gains come when groups are between two and four and that there are academic *losses* when the group is larger than four (Marzano, 2007, p. 40). For many types of cooperative learning, Marzano believes that pairs or triads work best (2007, p. 40). It has been found that two people can work together more intuitively, while a greater number requires more preparation ("2 People," 2010).

◆ Groups should seldom be formed based on ability (Marzano, 2001, p. 86). On the few occasions when teachers might want to have advanced students work on a special project, or when some students need to be "retaught" a concept, then an ability-based group might make sense. But in the vast majority of time cooperative learning calls for heterogeneous groups (Johnson & Johnson, 1988).

Cooperative learning often works best when the teacher forms groups strategically—who might be able to draw out whom, who could benefit from getting to know another person, or who are two people who definitely should not be paired because of a recent conflict.

Group formation might also depend on the time of the day and the mood of the class. If you are going to do a quick think-pair-share activity, you could just have students talk to the person next to them. However, if the class mood is "sleepy," then you might want to assign partners that force students to move out of their seats.

◆ Use cooperative learning groups as an opportunity for leadership development. Have brief, private conversations with certain students telling them that you believe they are leaders (while pointing out that leadership is a quality they will need to accomplish the goals they have identified—see Question 1—and you would like them to be a leader in their groups). Ask them to be responsible for drawing others out, for making sure the group moves along, etc. Do this at least once with everybody in class during the year, and try to "debrief" and evaluate with them individually after they do it (or the next day).

Use cooperative learning groups as an opportunity for leadership development.

♦ Think strategically about where you want the groups to sit and how long you want students to be in the same group. These two elements are related. You might want to assign two or three students to be in the same group for several weeks to work on one long project, or have the same group meet for one week in the same location to work on various cooperative learning activities—some that might take a few minutes and some that might take a day or two.

Having regular assigned locations makes the transition to small groups go more smoothly, and it allows the teacher to place certain students away from other students who have a history of distracting each other. Create a small group seating chart that you change regularly.

♦ Explain clear assignment instructions and behavioral expectations verbally and in writing—before students divide into groups. When explaining the assignment instructions, be careful not to overwhelm students with too many instructions at once. If one part of the overall assignment will take thirty minutes, it might make sense to wait to explain the next step until students are ready. By leaving the instructions and behavioral expectations on the overhead or whiteboard, teachers just have to point to them in response to certain student questions.

Behavioral expectations could include:

• "Please speak only with your partner(s)."

• "Please move the desks so that you are facing each other."

• "Lean-in" is a guideline recommended by Kelly Young at Pebble Creek Labs. We all tend to be more alert, awake, and attentive if we are "leaning-in" to the person with whom we are working with or talking to, as opposed to leaning back. In fact, researchers have found that "high-power poses," including leaning forward, can increase a person's sense of *feeling powerful* (as measured by self-reporting and chemical tests). "Low-power poses," including looking downward with hands on one's lap, can increase a person's sense of *powerlessness* (Hilo, 2010).

- "Please speak in lower voice."
- "Everyone should be working within ninety seconds" and then do a countdown.
- If students need to get materials, say "Each group should have one person go get the materials."

It would be useful to periodically model these listed behaviors or, better yet, have students model both the appropriate and inappropriate ones. These could be humorous moments that could also serve as important reminders.

If necessary, it might help to use the point system described in Question 4: How Do You Regain Control of an Out-of-Control Class? at the beginning of the school year during small group activities until students gain more experience.

♦ Have a teacher "sign" that means students should immediately stop their work and look at the teacher, and make sure that all students know what it is and what it means. There will periodically be times during cooperative learning when the teacher will want to clarify a point, highlight a student example on the overhead, or give further instructions. Having a standard procedure for that will make the activity go much more smoothly. For example, even just a teacher raising his/her hand and saying, "Can I have you attention, please?" can work well if students understand its purpose. When explaining this procedure, a teacher could say something like, "I love working in small groups, and I know a lot of you do, too. It's a lot better than you just having to sit there while I talk. But to make these small groups work, sometimes I will need to get your attention to give you further instructions or just check in. This is what I'm going to do. Let's practice it."

♦ The teacher should always be circulating as the small groups are working, The teacher needs to be answering questions, making sure that students are on the right track, and monitoring that everyone is "pulling their weight." One idea is to tell students that they will be assessed in two ways—individually and collectively.

Cooperative Learning Strategies

Think-Pair-Share or Think-Write-Pair-Share

This may be the most common example of cooperative learning used in classrooms today, and lends itself well to responding to higher-order questions and maximizing class participation.

It involves a teacher posing a question to the class, but prefacing it by saying that the teacher does not want students to say anything yet. Instead, he wants them to take a minute to think about their response. Often, the teacher can explain to students that writing can help us think more deeply and clearly and help us clarify what we want to say, so that he wants students to take a few minutes to write their response down on a piece of paper. By having students write, it also gives the teacher the opportunity to walk around and identify good work and help students who are having difficulties.

After explaining writing not only helps us clarify our thoughts, but talking about them does, too, the teacher can ask students to get with a partner (either an assigned one that requires them to move or someone next to them) and share what they wrote. Before students begin to share, however, remind students of the process and behavioral expectations. For example, the teacher might say:

> I'm going to have you get with your partner and share what you wrote. You can decide who can go first, and I would like each partner to ask one question after the other is done. Ideally, the questions will be one of the higher-order questions on the Revised Bloom's Taxonomy we studied. Please only speak with your partner—you have twenty seconds to get your desk facing him or her and to begin talking, and you'll have five minutes. Go!

The teacher can circulate while these discussions are going on, and identify students who he would like to share with the class (letting them know so they are prepared). That does not mean the teacher will not call on others, too, but setting up good student models to go first helps set a tone for the discussion. The teacher should not wait for everybody to be done, but instead should wait until most are finished. Having many students wait for a handful is an invitation to off-task behavior. Another option is to have a second question ready for those who are done early.

The teacher can tell students when they have one minute left, and then begin calling on students to share both their responses and, if they had been instructed to ask questions, what question they had been asked by their partner and what was their response. Including the task of having students ask their partners a question about what each has shared can add another level of engagement. At some point prior to this kind of activity, where the teacher instructs students to ask questions that would "require their partner to think," it would be important to provide scaffolded instruction on what that means. One way would be to offer examples of "good" and "bad" questions, possibly using the concept of attainment to make the distinction clear (see concept attainment examples in earlier chapters).

Of course, there also will be times when a teacher wants to do a much shorter version of a "think-pair-share." On those occasions, a teacher can just say: "I'd like you to think about a response to this question: _____. Take a minute to think…Now turn to your neighbor and quickly share your response."

This would be followed by a class discussion.

Jigsaw

Jigsaw is the common term used to describe a process whereby students become "experts" in a portion of a broader topic, and then join with other students who have become "experts" in other portions of the same topic. Each student then becomes a teacher to the others and shares their knowledge.

This process is most commonly used to read portions of a longer text, but could also be adapted for longer projects. For example, groups could research different aspects of a person's biography, the different causes of a war, or types of natural disasters.

One way to use the Jigsaw process is as follows:

1. The teacher identifies three or four components of the main topic. For example, the teacher could divide a reading into three or four parts (numbered one, two, three, four).

2. The teacher "numbers off" the class into ones, twos, threes, and fours or more (depending on the number of different reading sections).

   Each student silently reads the section assigned to their number (students in Group One would read section one, etc.). Each student develops a draft lesson that the student can teach individually. The teacher provides the outline for the lesson and perhaps a simple graphic organizer to complete. The outline/graphic organizer could include listing the three main ideas of their section of the article, how they could connect the information to other content they have learned, key quotes, a drawing, and questions they might have.

   Then each student meets with students of the same number. These are the "expert" groups—the ones who will become versed well enough in their sections so that they can teach them. It is best if the teacher has made arrangements with one student in each group to function as the leader.

Students could quickly share their draft lesson with their small group, and then each one could finalize the lesson they would teach, incorporating the best ideas from everyone. This lesson could include preparing a poster, and they might even rehearse it. Because each of the "expert" groups of students might be large, it would also be possible to "subdivide" it even further so that Groups One, Two, Three, and Four can be broken up into smaller "expert" groups of three or four students and follow the same process.

3. After each "expert" group is ready, each student returns to their original group and teaches their component. Students are challenged to ask questions to each presenter.

Project-Based Learning & Problem-Based Learning

There are many different types of more ambitious cooperative learning strategies. This chapter, however, briefly touches on just two that are related to each other—project-based learning and problem-based learning ("Project Based Learning," n.d.).

Project-based learning is typically defined as students working on a task that results in a concrete project (report, online slideshow, PowerPoint, poster, etc.) and/or public presentation. Problem-based learning can also result in a similar product, but the topic is generally a real-world problem that students must solve. Either strategy can take anywhere from a few days to a few weeks to complete (Prince & Felder, 2007).

Project-based learning topics might include role-playing a famous trial in history, relating the Black Death to modern science, or organizing a Veterans Day event at school ("Exemplary Projects," n.d.).

Problem-based learning assignments could include designing a human settlement on Mars, examining how the school lunchroom can be more efficiently organized, or having students encourage greater participation in the U.S. Census by neighborhood residents.

Ed Tech: Collaborative Storytelling

 Collaborative storytelling is an activity where one person begins telling a story, and then various others continue and complete it. It can be a fun and quick cooperative learning exercise. There are quite a few online tools that a designed to make this kind of collaborative storytelling much easier to do online, including letting you create private groups that only let people you choose participate in the story creation. A list of these sites can be found at http://larryferlazzo.edublogs.org/2010/12/29/the-best-sites-for-collaborative-storytelling/.

There are many topics that could fit into either one of these categories, such as the lesson plan attached to this chapter that challenges students to determine which neighborhood they think is best and that they would live in. It is designed to have students, particularly those living in urban areas, look at the "assets" in their community as opposed to the "deficits." In the unit plan, students identify what they believe are the most important qualities of a "good" neighborhood, use them as criteria to compare their area with a more affluent one, write a short persuasive essay explaining which neighborhood they think is better (the vast majority of students—if not all of them—typically choose their own), and then design an ideal neighborhood. Because the point of the activity is not to say their local neighborhood is perfect, an optional extension of this lesson is to identify ways students can work to make their area more like their "ideal" community.

The lesson plan provides one model for this kind of ambitious cooperative learning strategy. Many problem- and project-based learning plans have the same small group working together in all aspects of the lesson. This one, however, has students working alone, in larger small groups, and in pairs at different points.

The plan is designed for an Intermediate English class. However, several extensions are listed that make it appropriate for any class level, and the lesson design is a model for any project- or problem-based learning unit. More resources can be found at http://larryferlazzo.edublogs.org/2010/04/02/the-best-sites-for-cooperative-learning-ideas/.

Neighborhood Comparison Lesson Plan

Instructional Objectives

Students Will:

1. Identify what qualities they value in a neighborhood.

2. Students will use those qualities to compare their neighborhood with another neighborhood, perhaps one that is more affluent.

3. Students will write a persuasive essay explaining why one neighborhood is better than the other, most likely choosing their neighborhood as the better one.

4. Students will design their ideal neighborhood and write a description of it.

5. Multiple possible extensions to this lesson are listed. Doing any of them would add new instructional objectives.

Duration

Ten consecutive 55-minute periods

Common Core English Language Arts Standards

Reading:

1. Determine central ideas or themes of a text and analyze their development; summarize the key supporting details and ideas.

Writing:

1. Produce clear and coherent writing in which the development, organization, and style are appropriate to task, purpose, and audience.

2. Use technology, including the Internet, to produce and publish writing and to interact and collaborate with others.

Speaking & Listening:

1. Prepare for and participate effectively in a range of conversations and collaborations with diverse partners, building on others' ideas and expressing their own clearly and persuasively.

2. Adapt speech to a variety of contexts and communicative tasks, demonstrating command of formal English when indicated or appropriate.

Language:

1. Demonstrate command of the conventions of standard English grammar and usage when writing or speaking.

2. Demonstrate command of the conventions of standard English capitalization, punctuation, and spelling when writing.

Materials

1. Computer projector and Internet access

2. Student copies of "Important Qualities of a Neighborhood" (Figure 11.1, page 161), "Neighborhood Research Sheet" (Figure 11.2, page 162), "Neighborhood Field Trip Checklist (Figure 11.3, page 163), "Design Your Ideal Neighborhood" (Figure 11.4, page 164), and maps of each of the two neighborhoods (http://maps.google.com/)

3. Access to a computer lab for all students for two class periods

4. Poster paper and color markers

5. A manila folder for each student

Procedure

NOTE: At least two weeks prior to beginning this unit, the teacher should make arrangements for a field trip to either one or both of the neighborhoods. Be sure to arrange for student permission slips.

First Day

1. The teacher asks students to think for a minute and write down one thing they like about their neighborhood. After a minute, students share what they wrote with a partner, and the teacher asks for students to call out what they wrote. As students say them, the teacher writes them down on an easel paper or document camera.

2. The teacher explains that the class is going to begin a two-week project where students will compare two neighborhoods—theirs and the richest neighborhood in town—and decide which one is best. They will also design their vision of an ideal neighborhood.

3. The teacher distributes copies of "Important Qualities of A Neighborhood" (Figure 11.1, page 161) to each student, and asks them to rate each listed quality, and list others they think are important (they can use the list the class generated earlier for ideas). After several minutes, students are divided into pairs and told that they will be doing much, but not all, of the entire project together with that partner. Partners should share what they each wrote and try to develop a common list.

4. The teacher asks students to share any new qualities that are not on the class list already. As she adds them to the list, she tells students that, if they want, they can add them to their list, too, but only if they think they are important.

5. Next, the teacher asks students to put all the items they rated as either "A Little Important" or "Very Important" into one of three categories: Money, People, or Services (this is an example of inductive learning).

6. Teacher gives all students a folder and asks them to label it "Neighborhood Project." She explains that they should place all their materials for this unit in the folder, and that they should leave the folder in the classroom. She asks a student to be responsible for distributing the folders at the beginning of each class period and collecting them at the end.

7. Teacher shows a map of the school neighborhood on the document camera, and then shows a copy of the "Neighborhood Research Sheet" (Figure 11.2, page 162). She reviews the sheet, pointing out the class will be going to the computer lab the next day, and that they need to go to the indicated websites to find the information. She uses the computer projector to model

how to use the sites to find the information. She also explains that students should list other information they think is important that they learn about their neighborhood. The teacher might also consider setting up a blog or website with the links already there, or even using one that is already in place ("Neighborhood Research," 2010).

Second Day

1. The teacher brings students to the computer lab to research data on the school neighborhood's zip code. Students can work alone or with their partner.

2. The teacher explains that the class will be going on a walking tour of their neighborhood using the "Neighborhood Filed Trip Checklist" (Figure 11.3, page 163), which she reviews. She explains that students should be in groups of four on the field trip, so that each of their partner pairs should team up with another pair. While students are walking and completing the checklist, they should be taking photos with their cellphones. All students will be uploading them to a common site (see http://larryferlazzo. edublogs.org/2010/08/11/the-best-web-applications-that-lets-multiple-people-upload-their-photos-to-one-site/) the next time they visit the computer lab, or they can do it from home. The teacher shows students their route on the overhead/document camera.

Third Day

1. Students go on walking tour of their neighborhood.

Fourth Day

1. Students take out the "data set" of qualities they had identified as important to them in a neighborhood, and, with a color pencil, put a check mark next to the qualities they found present in the walking tour.

2. The teacher shows students a map of the more affluent neighborhood, and explains that they are going to the computer lab to research the same questions they did on the school neighborhood.

3. Students are given another copy of the "Neighborhood Research Sheet" and, either working alone or in pairs, find the information.

4. The teacher reviews the route of their next day's field trip to the affluent neighborhood (another option for either of the field trips is to do it "virtually" using Google Maps "Street View"; see http://maps.google.com/).

Fifth Day

1. Students either go on a field trip to the more affluent neighborhood using the same Checklist, or the teacher uses a computer projector to lead the class on a virtual tour while students complete the checklist.

Sixth Day

1. Students take out the "data set" of qualities they had identified as important to them in a neighborhood, and with a different color pencil than they used for the school neighborhood, put a checkmark next to the qualities they found present in the more affluent neighborhood.

2. The teacher then asks students to fold a sheet of paper in half and write the zip code of their neighborhood on the top of one column and the other zip code on the other side. Students are then asked to list the important neighborhood qualities they found in each neighborhood using the color coding on their sheets. Student pairs then meet to compare their charts. The school neighborhood typically has a much longer list than the other one.

3. Students then begin work on their own to write a persuasive essay saying which neighborhood is better. Teachers can find support materials, including essay outlines at these two sites: http://larryferlazzo.edublogs. org/2009/11/14/the-best-online-resources-for-helping-students-learn-to-write-persuasive-essays/ and http://larryferlazzo.edublogs.org/2008/ 01/11/the-best-websites-for-k-12-writing-instructionreinforcment/.

Seventh Day

1. Students continue working on their persuasive essay. If possible or desired, students could visit a computer lab and upload their essays onto a class blog where other students could read and comment on them. Students could also use their field trip photos to create a multimedia presentation. (Resources to help students learn how to create these kinds of presentations can be found at http://larryferlazzo.edublogs.org/2009/05/25/the-best-sources-of-advice-for-making-good-presentations/.)

Eighth Day

1. The teacher explains that students are now going to design their own ideal neighborhood. They can work alone, or with their assigned partner. The teacher can review the student handout (Figure 11.4, page 164) and also show a simple model neighborhood she drew.

2. Students begin work on their neighborhood.

Ninth Day

1. Students complete their ideal neighborhood and write their very short "essay" (two paragraphs) either alone or with a partner. The teacher could expand this into a full-fledged essay, if desired.

2. The teacher explains that students will have part of the following day to complete their design and essay, and that the last portion of the day will be spent "speed-dating" (having students line up across from each other) and having students present their neighborhoods. Each student should also ask at least one question of the presenting pair.

Tenth Day

1. Students complete their ideal neighborhood and essay and practice their presentation.

2. Students present to each other.

Assessment

Teachers can create a detailed rubric appropriate for their classroom situation assessing writing, public speaking, and cooperation. Free online resources to both find premade rubrics and to create new ones can be found at http://larryferlazzo.edublogs.org/2010/09/18/the-best-rubric-sites-and-a-beginning-discussion-about-their-use/.

Possible Extensions/Modifications

(More details on how to implement these extensions/modifications can be found at http://larryferlazzo.edublogs.org/2010/02/25/a-lesson-highlighting-community-assets-not-deficits/.)

Students could:

1. Read about fictional neighborhoods in literature.

2. Listen to songs about neighborhoods and write their own.

3. Create infographics using data on the different neighborhoods

4. Review what the Gallup Poll, in their major "Soul of the Community" study of twenty-six areas, found to be the most common attributes of a "good" neighborhood. Then they could compare the Gallup Poll attributes with what they chose and discuss the differences.

5. Review what urban planners have identified as the qualities that make a "good" neighborhood and have students compare them with they chose and discuss the differences.

6. Students could identify elements in their "ideal" neighborhood that are missing from their local community and organize efforts to make local improvements.

Ed Tech: Sister Classes

Teachers can connect with a "sister class" in the United States or in a different country. Both classes can do a neighborhood project, and share multimedia presentations on their neighborhoods with each other. More information on how to connect with other classes can be found at http://larryferlazzo.edublogs.org/2009/05/30/the-best-ways-to-find-other-classes-for-joint-online-projects/.

Figure 11.1. Important Qualities in a Neighborhood

Rate each quality: 1 = Not Important; 2 = A Little Important; 3 = Very Important

Write a sentence explaining why you gave it that rating. (*Example:* If you rated "Parks are nearby" as a "3" you could write: "I gave this a 3 because my family goes to play in parks a lot.")

You may add other qualities.

1. Ethnic diversity. _____

2. Easy to get to places by bus or light rail. _____

3. Housing is affordable. _____

4. Churches are nearby. _____

5. Parks are nearby. _____

6. Stores are nearby. _____

7. Schools are nearby. _____

8. Many people who share your ethnicity live in the neighborhood. _____

9. Grocery stores that sell your ethnic food are nearby. _____

10.

11.

12.

Figure 11.2. Neighborhood Research Sheet

Zip Code _____

PEOPLE:

1. What are the ethnicities of people who live there? (ZIPSkinny—http://zipskinny.com/)

　　White _____%

　　Latino _____%

　　African American _____%

　　Asian _____%

　　Pacific Islander _____%

2. What is the median age of people who live there? _____ (HOTPADS—http://hotpads.com/)

SERVICES:

1. How many parks are there? _____ (HOTPADS—http://hotpads.com/)

2. How many schools are there? (ZIPSkinny—http://zipskinny.com/)

　　Elementary Schools _____

　　Middle Schools _____

　　High Schools _____

　　Colleges _____

MONEY:

1. What is the median rent? (HOTPADS http://hotpads.com/)

2. Write down the purchase prices of the last ten homes sold. (Local Newspaper Database)

OTHER: Write down any other information about this neighborhood that you think is interesting or would fit into your data set:

Figure 11.3. Neighborhood Field Trip Checklist

Name: _____

Burbank Neighborhood	Fabulous 40s
Places where people live: Check every time you see: A house _____ A duplex _____ An apartment _____ A trailer or trailer park _____	Places where people live: Check every time you see: A house _____ A duplex _____ An apartment _____ A trailer or trailer park _____
Pick one house and answer these questions: Is this house: big _____, medium _____, small _____. Does it have a fence around it? Yes _____ No _____ Chain link _____ Wood _____ Other kind of fence _____ How many windows does it have? _____ Are the windows barred? _____ What do you like about this house?	Pick one house and answer these questions: Is this house: big _____, medium _____, small _____. Does it have a fence around it? Yes _____ No _____ Chain link _____ Wood _____ Other kind of fence _____ How many windows does it have? _____ Are the windows barred? _____ What do you like about this house?
Commercial places: Check when you see A food store _____ An ethnic food store _____ A clothes store _____ A restaurant _____ A health service _____	Commercial places: Check when you see A food store _____ An ethnic food store _____ A clothes store _____ A restaurant _____ A health service _____
Other commercial: What do you see that you like?	Other commercial: What do you see that you like?
Check when you see: A bus stop _____ Light rail _____	Check when you see: A bus stop _____ Light rail _____

From Ferazzo, L. (2010). *English Language Learners: Teaching Strategies that Work.* Santa Barbara, CA: Linsworth. Copyright © 2010

Figure 11.4. Design Your Ideal Neighborhood

Using the information you learned on the field trip, the "Neighborhood Qualities" sheet you completed before the field trip, and what you learned researching the two neighborhoods on the computer, you must design your ideal neighborhood.

It must show at least several blocks, and you may tape two sheets together if you would like to make it bigger. Your map must include a map "key."

You may work alone or with a partner. If you want to work with a partner you must use an easel-size sheet. If you work with a partner, you must make a rough draft before you get an easel sheet.

After you design your neighborhood, you must write an essay about your ideal neighborhood.

The first part must describe your neighborhood in detail. You must also have a section describing the people who would live there: Would there be ethnic diversity? Would there be a lot of young people? How much money would most families earn? You can use the list on the sheet you used in the computer lab.

The second part must explain why you designed your neighborhood the way you did.

What Are the Easiest Ways to Use Educational Technology in the Classroom?

People are always talking about integrating technology into lessons. I'm okay with that, but I want to make sure that it brings an obvious benefit to student learning beyond what we can do with pen and paper in the classroom. And I want to be able to do it without me having to learn a whole lot of new technical skills. I'm not sure what I can do that would meet both criteria.

Just because something can be done using technology does not mean that it automatically enhances student learning. The ideas listed in this chapter, however, have the combined benefit of both requiring minimal new technical skills *and* providing a clearly valued-added benefit to student learning.

These ideas can benefit *all* students. The author's blog (http:// larryferlazzo.edublogs.org/) shares many more ways to use technology specifically with English Language Learners (the same blog also shares more complex ways to integrate technology into student learning). It is possible that some of the websites listed in this chapter may no longer be operating by the time you read this book. In addition, new sites may be offering additional learning opportunities. To be kept up-to-date on these kinds of developments, readers can periodically check a post at the author's blog (http://larryferlazzo.edublogs.org/2010/06/28/my-best-posts-for-tech-novices-plus-one-from-somebody-else/) where reports on new technology that meet the two criteria—being very easy to use and providing value-added benefit to student learning—are regularly updated.

In addition to the author's blog and the ideas listed in this chapter, teachers can easily connect "virtually" with colleagues from throughout the world for free professional development on any classroom question or idea, whether it is technology related or not. Classroom 2.0 (http://www.classroom20.com/), the English Companion Ning (http://englishcompanion.ning.com/), and EFL Classroom 2.0 (http://eflclassroom.ning.com/) are three of the largest online teacher communities. No matter what your level of competence in technology is, and no matter how many years of experience you have in the classroom, the welcoming atmosphere and talent on these sites can offer great opportunities for professional development.

This chapter is divided into three parts: "Very Easy Ways to Integrate Technology in the Classroom," "Easy Ways to Integrate Technology in the Classroom," and "How Should Students Work with Computers?" The second part provides ideas that are slightly more involved than the ones listed in the first part. However, if you feel comfortable using the tools listed in the first part, you should have no problem moving on to the second series of ideas. The last section contains a few suggestions on how to work with students when they are using computers—either in a computer lab or on laptops in the classroom.

Very Easy Ways to Integrate Technology in the Classroom

Using a Computer Projector

Computer projectors, which let you easily show images from your computer onto a screen, are increasingly being used in U.S. classrooms. One simple benefit for teachers is being able to easily show video clips without having to deal with a VCR/DVD projector, or the small size of a TV screen. Using a computer projector vastly increases the number of easily accessible video clips for all subject areas, even if you eliminate YouTube because it is blocked by most school content filters. It also allows you to show computer presentations developed by students and online learning games that can be played by the entire class.

Using a Document Camera

Eliminating the need to make transparencies is every teachers' dream if they've been using an overhead projector, and a document camera does the trick. Assuming the teacher also has a computer projector, a document camera lets you project anything you place beneath it (a small object, a sheet of paper, a book page) onto a screen. Being able to have students bring their work up to easily show good models to the class is a great teaching tool.

Easily Creating an Authentic Audience for Student Work

Students can be much more engaged in, and committed to, what they are writing/creating for class if they know the audience is for more than just the teacher. Here are some easy ways to make this happen:

To Make It Easily Viewable by Other Classmates

Any document, including one in Microsoft Word, can be quickly uploaded to the Internet with a free application like Crocodoc (http://crocodoc.com/) or TxtBear (http://www.txtbear.com/), neither of which requires registration. All you do is click on your file and seconds letter you're given an URL address for it. Once you have that, though, what do you do with it to make it accessible?

There are two very easy options. One is by simply creating a free blog from Edublogs (http://edublogs.org/) (as that is the blog host that is least likely to be blocked by school content filters) and having students paste the URL addresses of their own creations to the blog as a comment. Other students can leave comments in the same area making observations about their classmate's posts. Or they can just write them on a piece of paper to share. Kidblogs (http://kidblog.org/home.php) is another option.

A second option is to have each student e-mail their creation's URL address to the teacher. The teacher can then copy and paste the URLs into something like Dinky Page (http://www.dinkypage.com/), a supereasy website creation tool that doesn't even require registration. Similar sites include Twextra (http://twextra.com/index.php), Just Paste It (http://justpaste.it/), and Axess (http://axess.im/). You can also use a site like Posterous (http://posterous.com/), which allows you to e-mail what you want to appear on your website without even having to go set it up.

To Make It Easily Viewable by Others Beyond the Classroom

There are many places where students can easily copy and paste what they have created for class so that others throughout the world can read it. Students can become excited at the possibility, and their level of commitment can increase. A few of the many potential places for students to place what they write (with no added work required from the teacher) follow.

Timelines (http://timelines.com/) lets users contribute towards making "timelines" of historical events with text, photos, and videos. People can then vote on which ones they like best, though everyone's contributions remain displayed. It is extremely easy to contribute—and much, much easier than adding to Wikipedia. Google's Knol (http://knol.google.com/) is another easy place to use for the same purpose.

Students can write book reviews at Shelfari (http://www.shelfari.com/) and Library Thing (http://www.librarything.com/).

They can decide a question they want to learn the answer to, post it on one of numerous question/answer websites, and research and write the answer (or pick a question that is already there). Good sites for this activity include Yahoo Answers (http://answers.yahoo.com/), WikiAnswers (http://wiki.answers.com/), and Wikianswers (http://answers.wikia.com/wiki/Wikianswers)—yes, the last two are indeed different sites.

The BBC's "A History Of The World" (http://www.bbc.co.uk/ahistoryoftheworld/explorerflash/#/object_li6X6vc1SMSJfJ2BhOdB0A) is an interactive timeline display of historical objects with images and commentary. Not only is it an accessible and engaging way to learn more about world history, but after a quick site registration users can contribute your own historical object choice to the collection and write about it.

Students can write commentary about current events at any online website—local, national, or international. The *New York Times* also has a "Student Opinion" site (http://learning.blogs.nytimes.com/category/student-opinion/) to create a "safe space on NYTimes.com—and on the Internet overall—for students 13 and older to voice their views on the news."

Spotery (http://www.spotery.com/) is somewhat similar; users can leave comments on news stories from around the Web. It differs, though, in one key way that makes it potentially especially engaging to students—users can add a link to the site or to any other article about a topic that they are interested in. Then, they can leave a comment about that news item. Or, a teacher can choose a particular article that the teacher wants students to comment on and, in addition to student comments, can check to see what other people have said, too. Brikut (http://www.brikut.com/) is a similar site.

These are just a few of the literally hundreds of unique sites on the Web where students can post their writing so that it can be viewed by others. More possibilities are listed at http://larryferlazzo.edublogs.org/2009/04/01/the-best-places-where-students-can-write-for-an-authentic-audience/ and http://larryferlazzo.edublogs.org/2009/04/04/the-best-places-where-students-can-create-online-learningteaching-objects-for-an-authentic-audience/.

Annotating the Web

Many teachers encourage students to demonstrate their use of reading strategies through the use of highlighting, sticky notes, or actual writing on the margins. Students can do the same with online material. Webklipper (http://webklipper.com/) and Crocodoc (http://crocodoc.com/) let students do the same thing on any webpage with a virtual highlighter, sticky note, and drawing tool. An individual student can make his/her annotations, or multiple students can use the same page. It's free and no registration is required. You're given an URL address for the annotated page. In fact, any document can be uploaded to Crocodoc, converted into a webpage, and be annotated by one and all. This lets all students see examples from their classmates. Bounce (http://www.bounceapp.com/) is a similar application.

Engaging Reluctant Readers

NewsCred (http://newscred.com/) and icurrent (http://www.icurrent.com/frontpage) are two simple places where students can create their own personalized daily newspapers that only include content on topics that interest them. They are attractively designed and easy to use. Having their own newspapers certainly makes it harder for students to say that they can't find anything interesting to read! You can find other similar applications at http://larryferlazzo.edublogs.org/2010/04/11/the-best-sites-for-creating-personalized-newspapers-online/.

Searching the Web

Most search engines will function adequately for student research. However, some like Middlespot (http://middlespot.com/search.php) and Mel Zoo (http://www.melzoo.com/en_US/search) offer the additional advantage of providing images of the search results. That kind of visual support not only helps students with reading and other learning challenges, it can save time for any searcher by giving a clearer view of what might be on the page. A similar feature can now be activated in Google by clicking on the magnifying glass next to each regular search result.

Organizing Research

Many students need help developing organization skills, especially with research. Once students find potential websites that can be useful in their project(s), sites like Middlespot (http://middlespot.com/search.php), Wallwisher (http://www.wallwisher.com/), or Tizmos (http://www.tizmos.com/) can be easy "bookmarking" pages where students can save web pages for future reference. Not only are these three supersimple to use and free, but they also show the images of the saved sites, not just their names. Plus, unlike some of the more popular bookmarking applications, they tend not be blocked by school content filters.

Easy Ways to Integrate Technology in the Classroom

These are a few slightly more involved ways to use technology to bring value-added benefits to student learning.

Videotaping Student Presentations

Recording student presentations so they can be replayed and evaluated in a respectful way—first by the presenters themselves and then by others—can provide a huge learning benefit for students. Digital recorders like Flip Video cameras are relatively inexpensive, and can have numerous other uses. For more ideas, go to http://larryferlazzo.edublogs.org/2009/06/05/the-best-sources-for-advice-on-using-flip-video-cameras/.

Connecting With an Online Sister Class— Ideally in Another Country

It is relatively easy now to make that sort of connection. There are numerous websites specifically designed to help classes and schools develop relationships (see "The Best Ways to Find Other Classes for Joint Online Projects" at http://larryferlazzo.edublogs.org/2009/05/30/the-best-ways-to-find-other-classes-for-joint-online-projects/). And teachers can find relationships that are as loose or structured as they want. Some may have legitimate questions about the value-added benefit that products like VoiceThreads (http://voicethread.com/) (user-created audio slideshows) and other multimedia presentations (see http://larryferlazzo.edublogs.org/2008/05/06/the-best-ways-to-create-online-slideshows/) can offer to mainstream students (those who are not English Language Learners or who are not facing learning challenges). However, there is no question that these kinds of tools can provide that kind of benefit if done in the context of communicating and learning about different communities with peers from different cultures.

Participating in & Creating Virtual Field Trips

There are many great examples of "virtual field trips" that are available for free on the Web, as well as easy ways both teachers and students can create ones for their own class (and for others). You can learn more about these at "The Best Resources for Finding and Creating Virtual Field Trips" at http://larryferlazzo.edublogs.org/2009/08/11/the-best-resources-for-finding-and-creating-virtual-field-trips/. Virtual field trips can be integrated with whatever unit is being taught in the classroom and, with current budget restraints, it provides an alternative (although, admittedly, a weak one) to expensive "nonvirtual" ones.

There are many other ways in which technology can be used effectively in the classroom. They may be more complex than the ideas listed in this chapter, or they may arguably not hold an advantage over using "low-tech" or "no-tech" ways of accomplishing the same learning objectives in the classroom. Of course, using technology can also provide a periodic "change of pace" to students, which in itself could be a useful teaching strategy. In addition to the author's blog, another excellent site for exploring other effective technology uses is Educational Origami–Bloom's Digital Taxonomy (http://edorigami.wikispaces.com/Bloom's+Digital+Taxonomy). It provides in-depth guidance on how to use technology tools to promote higher-order thinking skills.

How Should Students Work with Computers?*

Here are some ideas to keep in mind when students are using computers to work on a project:

♦ Use computers more to *reinforce* key concepts, and less to *teach* them.

There are many learning activities that are available over the Internet. However, students cannot often ask the computer nuanced questions, and the computer cannot easily give nuanced answers. Computers do not recognize quizzical expressions on student faces. A "congratulations!" message from a computer program is not the same as a verbal acknowledgment from a smiling teacher. Students can learn many facts from a computer—learning concepts can be much more difficult. Computers do not necessarily teach ambiguity well.

An effective technique used to teach English Language Learners can be adapted for when students work with computers. The strategy is called "Preview, View, Review." In the bilingual ESL classroom, this means a short overview of the lesson is first given in the students' native language, followed by the lesson itself given in English, and ending with a short review time in the native language where questions can be answered as well.

Using this kind of "sandwich" method, with computer time in the middle and teacher-to-entire-class interaction on both ends, can work well in a computer lab class, too. Community organizers call this simple process "Planning, Action, Evaluation." Of course, the teacher should be constantly circulating and engaging students during the computer time, too, and not just sit at their own station.

---

* Portions of this section previously appeared in *TechLearning* and are reprinted with their permission.

♦ Computers can be used to help students develop and deepen relationships *with each other*, not just *with the computer screen*.

Redwood trees can grow alone. However, they do not grow as tall as redwoods that are growing in a grove together. When they are together, their roots connect underground and get intertwined. This connection allows them to grow taller by providing a much more solid base.

The same holds true with our students. Yes, students can learn something from just working on computers alone and, in effect, just developing a relationship with a monitor's screen. However, just like in the regular classroom, working together can create so many more possibilities and develop so many more skills (see Question 11, the cooperative learning chapter).

♦ Use time in the computer lab to help develop *leadership* among students, and not just have them be your *followers*.

Look for students who seem to be doing a particularly good job, or who seem to be grasping what to do technically quickly, and ask them if they would mind helping others. At the beginning of the year, alert students to this possibility and spend time talking about what the difference is between "guiding" someone and "doing it for them." Model examples, also.

♦ Spend less time being the *controller* and more time helping students develop *self-control*.

Yes, we need to be aware of what is on our student's screens. And, yes, we need to make sure our students are aware of how to behave near expensive equipment. However, having thoughtful class discussions prior to entering the lab or prior to working on laptops and engaging in reflective individual conversations when lapses occur tend to be much more effective in teaching life-long learning than harsh denunciations and punishments.

Technology is not a panacea for all classroom challenges. However, it can be a good supplement and an asset to a well-designed lesson. To paraphrase an unknown economist who was supposedly speaking about the free market:

Technology has its place, but also has to be kept in its place.

How Can You Best Use Learning Games in the Classroom?*

I know that students enjoy playing games in class, and I enjoy it, too! I'm concerned, though, that I'm not maximizing the learning opportunities they can provide. I'm just not sure what are the best kind to play, when to play them, and how exactly to structure them.

William Glasser identifies the need to have fun as one of our basic human needs and identifies learning something new as one way to fulfill that need (Glasser, 1988, p. 31). Of course, for many of us, it depends on what that "something new" is. Playing games can help students who might not value learning particular information or concepts as much as we might hope. Games can reinforce and review this content in an engaging way.

According to neuroscience researchers Renate and Geoffrey Caine, incorporating a sense of play in the classroom is one way (Caine & Caine, 1994, p. 145) we can also help students reach the state that neuroscience has identified as "relaxed alertness":

---

* Portions of this chapter were previously published in *English Language Learners: Teaching Strategies That Work*. Copyright ©2010 by ABC-CLIO, LLC, reproduced with permission of ABC-CLIO, LLC, and in *Language Magazine* (December, 2006), reprinted with permission.

People in a state of relaxed alertness experience low threat and high challenge...Essentially, the learner is both relaxed and to some extent excited or emotionally engaged at the same time...In this state, the learner feels competent and confident and has a sense of meaning or purpose. (Caine, 2009, pp. 12, 21)

Judy Willis, neurologist and teacher, writes that students, especially adolescents, are more likely to store information as part of their long-term memory and make them available for later retrieval through participating in activities they enjoy (Willis, 2006, p. 20).

Robert Marzano reviewed 60 studies on using games in the classroom and found that if done well, using games increases student academic achievement by an average of 20%. He suggests that important characteristics of an effective learning game include letting them have "low-stakes" (simple prizes with no grade consequences), including key academic content, using the game as an opportunity to identify and review essential information that students might not have learned, and giving students time to reflect on what they might have learned from the game (Marzano, 2010).

In addition to Marzano's criteria for a learning game, here are a few others to consider:

1. It requires no or extremely minimal preparation on the teacher's part.

2. Most needed materials are developable by the students themselves— the preparation for the games can be a learning experience in itself.

3. In addition to not costing teachers much time, it can be done without costing any money.

4. The game is designed in a way that strongly encourages all students in the class to be engaged at all times.

5. The game, after being modeled by the teacher a number of times, periodically also can be led by a student.

Although this chapter focuses on ideas for easy "overt" learning games, studies show that "framing" certain class activities as "fun" can have a positive effect for students who might ordinarily be considered "low-achieving" (DiSalvo, 2010, August 24). For example, describing clozes (fill-in-the-blanks), sequencing activities, and categorizing inductive data sets (all which were written about in previous chapters) as "puzzles" can increase student interest in performing well.

This chapter has one section listing "low-tech" games and another that shares simple ways to incorporate computer technology. The second section focuses on using gaming technology in ways such that no previous tech experience is required. There are many examples of using technology for learning games and simulations that are far more involved than the ones listed here.

These include ones like Evoke (http://www.urgentevoke.com/), which was developed by the World Bank and where players can solve global challenges, and Peacemaker (http://www.peacemakergame.com/), where players have to bring peace to the Middle East. Edutopia (http://www.edutopia.org/) is a good resource to learn about these kinds of activities.

Though many "low-tech" and "high-tech" games in this chapter can be made accessible to English Language Learners, both the author's website (http://larryferlazzo.edublogs.org/) and the book, *English Language Learners: Teaching Strategies That Work* (Ferlazzo, 2010) have many more that are specifically targeted towards ELLs.

"Low-Tech" Games

Games Using Small Whiteboards

Having a few small, handheld whiteboards (along with markers and erasers or pieces of cloth) can make a number of games go smoothly, though pieces of scratch paper can act as substitutes.

Divide the class into small groups of two to four students (review the research in Question 11, the cooperative learning chapter). You can change how the groups are formed, sometimes allowing students to choose their own partners and at other times just have them "number off." However, always reserve the right to move students around if you believe that one group is too strong or weak.

One model entails calling out a question to answer (or the answer and students having to write the question), giving the groups 20 or 30 seconds to write the answer (and telling them not to raise their board until you say time is up), and then having them show the answer. The groups with the correct answer get a point. This way everyone has an opportunity to score a point, not just the first one with the answer. You can sometimes end this game, and others, with an opportunity for each team to bet all or part of their points on the last question (like in *Final Jeopardy*). Another option is for the teacher to make a list of common writing errors and write them on the board (obviously, without indicating which student wrote the mistake) and then have groups race to write them correctly. Both these versions can also be designed on a *Jeopardy* "board" using either a whiteboard, a sheet of paper shown on a document camera, or in an online version described in the next section.

Headline Clues (http://gel.msu.edu/headlineclues/game/) is a challenging online game from Michigan State University that can be adapted for the classroom. In it, players are shown the lead paragraph, but letters from two words in the headline are missing. Players have to use clues in the first paragraph to identify what the missing words should be. Once the teacher models several examples, students can create their own.

Games That Require Students to Create Materials

Sentence Scrambles can be a popular game. Students are given blank index cards, or they can just cut up pieces of paper. Each student picks one sentence from a book they have been reading (or any other piece of text) and writes the words and punctuation marks on the cards (one word and one punctuation mark per card). They mix up the cards and then paper clip them together. They then do the same for another sentence. Each student can create five. The teacher collects them, divides the class into small groups, and gives each group a stack of the sentence scrambles to put into the correct order. The group that has the most correct sentences in ten or fifteen minutes wins. After a group feels they have one sentence correct the teacher can go check it and take the sentence scramble away after giving them a point.

As described earlier, one inductive learning strategy is having students categorize data sets. Students can be asked to prepare categories using the content they have learned, briefly writing all the items they can that fit into those categories. Then, one student can slowly call out the items he/she has in the category, giving groups time to try and decide to which category the items belong. For example, a student could say "working in quarry," give groups thirty seconds to write down the appropriate category, and if no one does, move on to "playing soccer" and so on (the correct category in this case would be "Things that Nelson Mandela did while in prison" learned as part of a unit on his life).

Students can be asked to make a list of twenty review questions and their answers. Each student then takes a turn asking a question that all the small groups have to answer on their whiteboard. Students receive an automatic point when asking their question. However, students are told beforehand that if the teacher considers any question too easy, then the student asking the question will have to also answer a second question from the teacher in order to earn his/her point. To ensure that there are no repeated questions, the number of review questions to ask each student to write should be the same as the number of students in that class. In other words, if you have thirty students, have them write thirty review questions and answers.

Online Games

Games Where Teachers and/or Students Can Create the Content

There are many free online tools where teachers and, more importantly, students, can create games that their students (and, in the case of student-created games, classmates) can play. Multiple game templates already exist on the sites, and users need to add the questions (and answers) of their choice. The ones listed here are very similar—registration takes less than a minute, they are unlikely to be blocked by school content filters because they only contain educational games, and people who are not familiar with tech tools should be able to learn to use them within a minute or two (you can find additional sites at http://larryferlazzo.edublogs.org/2008/04/21/the-best-websites-for-creating-online-learning-games/):

- Class Tools (http://classtools.net/)
- Philologus (http://www.philologus.co.uk/index.php)
- Purpose Games (http://www.purposegames.com/)
- What 2 Learn (http://www.what2learn.com/)

The games created on these sites are also hosted there. Links to all the games created by students in a class can be easily posted on a class blog or website (see Question 12 on using technology). They can also be projected on a screen with a classroom computer projector, and the questions can be used in the "low-tech" games described in the previous section.

Games Where the Content has Already Been Created

There are numerous online games that already have content included, where students can play individually, against each other online, and/or in small groups as a class with the game projected on a screen. If these games include content that you have taught and would like students to review, or provide an engaging opportunity for them to apply some of that knowledge they have already gained, then they are worth considering using as a student activity. Here are a few examples (you can find many more at http://larryferlazzo.edublogs.org/2010/08/28/a-collection-of-the-best-lists-on-games/):

- Against All Odds (http://www.playagainstallodds.com/game_us.html) is an online game created by UNHCR, the United Nations High Commission for Refugees. In it, players simulate the role of a refugee in various scenarios.
- Electrocity (http://www.electrocity.co.nz/) is an award-winning game where players can create their own cities and see the environmental consequences of their design decisions.
- iCue (http://www.icue.com/) is a project of NBC News, and has numerous online interactives, including games, related to U.S. history, English, U.S. government, and environmental science.

Games can be a helpful supplement in the classroom. And, as Roland "Prez" Pryzbylewski, a teacher in the HBO television series, *The Wire*, said, in some circumstances games can be useful because you

"Trick them into thinking they aren't learning and they do."
—Roland "Prez" Prysbylewski, character in the HBO series
The Wire

Afterword

The challenges listed in this book, and the ideas that are offered as ways to respond, are just a "drop in the bucket" of the many issues that face classroom teachers and their students every day. If you have other challenges that you and your colleagues are confronting, share them at http://larryferlazzo. edublogs.org/contact-me/. If you have ideas on how you have effectively responded to some common classroom problems, please consider sharing them there, as well.

References

Allen, J. (2000). *Yellow brick roads*. Portland, ME: Stenhouse.

Arendt, H. (2006). *Eichmann in Jerusalem: A report on the banality of evil*. New York: Penguin Books.

Berten, H. (2008). *Peer influences on risk behavior: A network study of social influence on adolescents in Flemish secondary schools*. Paper presented at the Annual Meeting of the American Sociological Society, Boston. Retrieved from http://www.allacademic.com/meta/p_mla_apa_research_citation/2/3/9/7/8/p239786_index.html

Bronson, P. (2007, February 11). How not to talk to your kids: The inverse power of praise. *New York Magazine*. Retrieved from http://nymag.com/news/features/27840/

Bronson, P. (2010). Snooze or lose. *New York Magazine*. Retrieved from http://nymag.com/news/features/38951/index3.html#ixzz0eulnLtvT

Bryner, J. (2010, January 19). Workplace blame is contagious and detrimental. *Live Science*. Retrieved from http://www.livescience.com/culture/blame-contagious-100119.html

Caine, G. (2009). *Brain/mind learning principles in action*. Thousand Oaks, CA: Corwin Press.

Caine, R. N., & Caine, G. (1994). *Making connections: Teaching and the human brain*. Menlo Park, CA: Addison-Wesley.

Can stillness and reflection improve learning? (2010, January 17). *The Emotion Machine*. Retrieved from http://www.theemotionmachine.com/can-stillness-and-reflection-improve-learning

Carey, B. (2009, April 16). Task to aid self-esteem lifts grades for some. *The New York Times*. Retrieved from http://www.nytimes.com/2009/04/17/science/17esteem.html?_r=2

Carey, B. (2010, December 6). Tracing the spark of creative problem-solving. *The New York Times*. Retrieved from http://www.nytimes.com/2010/12/07/science/07brain.html?_r=2&ref=science

Chai, B. (2009, December 31). How to stay motivated—and get that bonus. *The Wall Street Journal*. Retrieved from http://online.wsj.com/article/SB10001424052748704152804574628230428869074.html

Cloze strategy summary. (n.d.). Pebble Creek Labs. Retrieved from http://pebblecreeklabs.com/instructional-strategies/cloze/183-cloze-strategy-summary.html

Cohen, G. L.; Garcia, J.; Purdie-Vaughns, V.; Apfel, N.; & Brzustoski, P. (2009). Recursive processes in self-affirmation: Intervening to close the minority achievement gap. *Science, 324*(5925), 400–403.

Couros, G. (2010, May 15). Bloom's taxonomy and a pen. *The principal of change: Stories of learning and leading.* Retrieved from http://georgecouros.ca/blog/archives/430

Deci, E. L. (1995). *Why we do what we do.* New York: Penguin Books.

Delayed school start time associated with improvements in adolescent behaviors. (2010, July 5). *E! Science News.* Retrieved from http://esciencenews.com/articles/2010/07/05/delayed.school.start.time.associated.with.improvements.adolescent.behaviors

DiSalvo, D. (2010, August 24). Slackers better at "fun" activities. *Scientific American.* Retrieved from http://www.scientificamerican.com/article.cfm?id=slackers-better-at-fun-activities

DiSalvo, D. (2010, January 10). Does making a public commitment really help people lose weight? *Neuronarrative.* Retrieved from http://neuronarrative.wordpress.com/2010/01/10/does-making-a-public-commitment-really-help-people-lose-weight/?utm_source=feedburner&utm_medium=feed&utm_campaign=Feed:+NEURONARRATIVE+(Neuronarrative)&utm_content=Google+Reader)

DiSalvo, D. (2010, March 11). When you expect rapid feedback, the fire to perform gets hotter. *Neuronarrative.* Retrieved from http://neuronarrative.wordpress.com/2010/03/11/when-you-expect-rapid-feedback-the-fire-to-perform-gets-hotter/?utm_source=feedburner&utm_medium=feed&utm_campaign=Feed:+ResearchBloggingNeuroscienceEnglish+(Research+Blogging+-+English+-+Neuroscience)&utm_content=Google+Reader)

Disappointed Bush fails as a role model. (2008). *Steve Young on politics.* Retrieved from http://steveyoungonpolitics.com/dissappointed-bush-fails-as-a-role-model/

Doyle, A. C. (2010). *The sign of the four.* London, England: Bibliolis Books.

Doyle, T. (n.d.). *Evaluating teacher effectiveness—Research summary.* Retrieved from http://www.ferris.edu/fctl/Teaching_and_Learning_Tips/Research%20on%20Students'%20Evalution%20of%20Faculty%20Teaching/EvalTeachEffec.htm

Drucker, P. (1974). *Management: Tasks, responsibilities, practices.* New York: Harper & Row.

Duckworth, A. (2010, January 14). Eureka! *Are We a Blog?* Retrieved from http://setiradio.blogspot.com/2010/01/eureka-angela-duckworth.html

Dunn, M. (2007). *Reading fluency: What, why, and how?* Retrieved from http://www.u-46.org/dbs/roadmap/files/newsletter/news-fluency4-07.pdf

Dweck, C. (2006). *Mindset: The new psychology of success.* New York: Ballantine.

Dweck, C. S. (2007). The perils and promise of praise. *Educational Leadership, 65*(2), 34–39. Retrieved from http://www.ascd.org/publications/educational-leadership/oct07/vol65/num02/The-Perils-and-Promises-of-Praise.aspx

Dweck, C. S. (2008, Winter). Brainology: Transforming students' motivation to learn. *School Matters.* Retrieved from http://www.nais.org/publications/ismagazinearticle.cfm?ItemNumber=150509

Dweck, C. S. (2010, September). Even geniuses work hard. *Educational Leadership*, *68*(1), 16–20. Retrieved from http://www.ascd.org/publications/educational-leadership/sept10/vol68/num01/Even-Geniuses-Work-Hard.aspx

Emerson, R. W. (n.d.). *Self-reliance*. Retrieved from http://www.emersoncentral.com/selfreliance.htm

Exemplary projects. (n.d.). *PBLnet.org*. Retrieved from http://www.wested.org/pblnet/exemplary_projects.html

Famous failures. (2007, July 30). *YouTube*. Retrieved from http://www.youtube.com/watch?v=dT4Fu-XDygw

Fast, N. J., & Tiedens, L. Z. (2010). Blame contagion: The automatic transmission of social psychology. *Journal of Experimental Social Psychology*, *46*, 97–106. Retrieved from http://www-bcf.usc.edu/~nathanaf/blame_contagion.pdf

Ferlazzo, L. (2010). *English language learners: Teaching strategies that work*. Santa Barbara, CA: Linworth.

Ferlazzo, L., & Hammond, L. A. (2009). *Building parent engagement in schools*. Santa Barbara, CA: Linworth.

Forehand, M. (2005). Bloom's taxonomy: Original and revised. In M. Orey (Ed.), *Emerging perspectives on learning, teaching, and technology*. Retrieved from http://projects.coe.uga.edu/epltt/index.php?title=Bloom's_Taxonomy

Frean, A. (2008, December 2). Google generation has no need for rote learning. *The Sunday Times*. Retrieved from http://www.timesonline.co.uk/tol/life_and_style/education/article5270092.ece

Gailliot, M. T. (2007, November). The physiology of willpower: Linking blood glucose to self-control. *Personality and Social Psychology Review*, *11*(4), 303–327. Retrieved from http://psr.sagepub.com/cgi/content/abstract/11/4/303

Gerstein, J. (2009, February 3). Obama on Daschle: I take responsibility. *Politico*. Retrieved from http://www.politico.com/news/stories/0209/18344.html

Glasser, W. (1988). *Choice theory in the classroom*. New York: Harper Perennial.

Glasser, W. (1998). *Choice theory: A new psychology of personal freedom*. New York: Harper Collins.

Glenn, D. (2010, May 9). Carol Dweck's Attitude: It's not about how smart you are. *The Chronicle of Higher Education*. Retrieved from http://chronicle.com/article/Carol-Dwecks-Attitude/65405/

Graff, G., & Birkenstein, C. (2009). *They say, I say: The moves that matter in academic writing*. New York: W. W. Norton.

Hampel, R. (2010, February 23). Should have, could have: What parents regret about high school. *Education Week*. Retrieved from http://www.edweek.org/ew/articles/2010/02/24/22hampel.h29.html?tkn=US%5bF8GLowkPh9GazSjcWe%2B4CUKRvQtS4F6%2B6&cmp=clp-edweek

Harvard Business School goal story. (2006, March 15). *Lifemastering*. Retrieved from http://www.lifemastering.com/en/harvard_school.html

Hatton, N., & Smith, D. (1995). Reflection in teacher education: Towards definition and implementation. *Teaching and Teacher Education*, *11*(1), 33–49.

Helliker, K. (2010, May 18). The power of a gentle nudge. *Wall Street Journal*. Retrieved from http://online.wsj.com/article/SB1000142405274870431490457525 0352409843386.html?mod=WSJ_LifeStyle_LeadStoryNA

Herbert, W. (2010, March 18). The power of gratitude. *We're only human*. Retrieved from http://www.psychologicalscience.org/onlyhuman/2010/03/power-of-gratitude.cfm

Higher-order thinking: Are students using higher order thinking operations within a critical framework? (2004). *Queensland Government, DET Education*. Retrieved from http://education.qld.gov.au/corporate/newbasics/html/ pedagogies/ intellect/int1a.html

Hilo, J. (2010, November 15). Power poses really work. *Miller-Mccune*. Retrieved from http://www.miller-mccune.com/culture-society/power-poses-really-work-25322/

Holmes, N. (2007). Mindset graphic. *Stanford Magazine*. Retrieved from http://www. stanfordalumni.org/news/magazine/2007/marapr/images/features/dweck/ dweck_mindset.pdf

Holt McDougal Literature for Texas, grade 9–12. (2010). *HMHEducation.com*. Retrieved from http://hmheducation.com/tx/lit912/authors_1.php

How taking an active role in learning enhances memory. (2010, December 6). *Science Daily*. Retrieved from http://www.sciencedaily.com/ releases/2010/12/101206111508.htm

How to improve your self-control. (2008, September 30). *Psyblog*. Retrieved from http://www.spring.org.uk/2008/09/how-to-improve-your-self-control.php

Hull, J. (2010, June 10). *A college degree does more than help your bank account*. The Center for Public Education. Retrieved from http://blog.centerforpubliceducation. org/?p=951

Inductive model summary. (n.d.). Retrieved from http://pebblecreeklabs.com/ instructional-strategies/inductive/180-inductive-model-summary.html

Jacobs, J. (2010, April 26). Motivating students via mental time travel. *Miller-McCune*. Retrieved from http://www.miller-mccune.com/culture-society/motivating-students-via-mental-time-travel-15122/

Jensen, E. (2000). *Brain-based learning*. San Diego: Brain Store.

Joachim Posada says, Don't eat the marshmallow yet. (2009, May). *TED: Ideas worth spreading*. Retrieved from http://www.ted.com/talks/joachim_de_posada_ says_don_t_eat_the_marshmallow_yet.html

Johnson, D. W., Johnson, R. T., & Roseth, C. (2006, March). Do peer relationships affect achievement? *The cooperative link*. Retrieved from http://www.co-operation. org/wp-content/uploads/2011/01/Volume-211.pdf

Johnson, R. T., & Johnson, D. W. (1988). Cooperative learning: Two heads are better than one. *In Context*. Retrieved from http://www.context.org/ICLIB/IC18/ Johnson.htm

Jones, J. (2010, September 21). Rewards—something to think about. *Care and Learning: An Ask Dr. Jami Blog*. Retrieved from http://careandlearning.org/resiliency/buildingresiliency.html/

Joseph, G. E., & Strain, P. S. (2006). *Helping young children control anger and handle disappointment*. Champaign, IL: University of Illinois at Urbana-Champaign, The Center on the Social and Emotional Foundations for Early Learning. Retrieved from http://www.behavioralinstitute.org/FreeDownloads/START/Help%20Young%20Chidren%20Control%20Anger%20Handle%20Disappointment.pdf

Joyce, B., & Calhoun, E. (1998). *Learning to teach inductively*. Boston: Allyn & Bacon.

Joyce, B., & Weil, M. (2009). *Models of teaching* (8th ed.). Boston: Pearson Education.

Kahneman, D. (2010, February). Daniel Kahneman: The riddle of experience vs memory. *TED*. Retrieved from http://www.ted.com/talks/lang/eng/daniel_kahneman_the_riddle_of_experience_vs_memory.html

Krathwohl, D. R. (2002). A revision of Bloom's taxonomy: An overview. *Theory Into Practice, 41*(4), 212–264.

Kristof, K. M. (2009, December 13). Break bad shopping habits to avoid debt hangover. *Los Angeles Times*. Retrieved from http://articles.latimes.com/2009/dec/13/business/la-fi-perfin13–2009dec13

Lack of morning light keeps teenagers up at night. (2010, February 27). *ScienceDaily*. Retrieved from http://www.sciencedaily.com/releases/2010/02/100216140305.htm

Lateral solution. (n.d.). Retrieved from http://brainyplanet.com/index.php/Lateral%20Solution

Latham, G. P., & Locke, E. A. (2006). Enhancing the benefits and overcoming the pitfalls of goal setting. *Organizational Dynamics, 35*(4), 332–340.

Lehrer, J. (2009, May 18). Don't! The secret of self-control. *The New Yorker*. Retrieved from http://www.newyorker.com/reporting/2009/05/18/090518fa_fact_lehrer?printable=true

Lehrer, J. (2009, August 2). The truth about grit. *The Boston Globe*. http://www.boston.com/bostonglobe/ideas/articles/2009/08/02/the_truth_about_grit/?page=1

Lehrer, J. (2009, October 22). Learning from mistakes. *The Science Blogs*. Retrieved from http://scienceblogs.com/cortex/2009/10/learning_from_mistakes.php

Lehrer, J. (2009, December 26). Blame it on the brain. *Wall Street Journal*. Retrieved from http://online.wsj.com/article/SB10001424052748703478704574612052322122442.html?mod=article-outset-box

Lehrer, J. (2010, April 19). Thinking about tomorrow. *The Science Blogs*. Retrieved from http://scienceblogs.com/cortex/2010/04/thinking_about_tomorrow.php?utm_source=feedburner&utm_medium=feed&utm_campaign=Feed:+ScienceblogsChannelBrain+(ScienceBlogs+Channel+:+Brain+%26+Behavior)&utm_content=Google+Reader)

Leonhardt, D. (2010, July 27). The case for $320,000 kindergarten teachers. *The New York Times*. Retrieved from http://www.nytimes.com/2010/07/28/business/economy/28leonhardt.html?_r=2&hp

Lewis, R., Romi, S., Qui, X., & Katz, Y. J. (2005). Teachers' classroom discipline and student misbehavior in Australia, China and Israel. *Teaching & Teacher Education, 21*(6), 729–741. Retrieved from http://www.sciencedirect. com/science?_ob=ArticleURL&_udi=B6VD8–4GMS97B-1&_user=10&_ coverDate=08/31/2005&_rdoc=1&_fmt=high&_orig=search&_ origin=search&_sort=d&_docanchor=&view=c&_acct=C000050221&_ version=1&_urlVersion=0&_userid=10&md5=e0fb6b03c473cabb58004f9f744b1e 6b&searchtype=a

Lippi take responsibility for failure. (2010, June 25). *Ninensm.* Retrieved from http:// wwos.ninemsn.com.au/article.aspx?id=1075741

Mahto, A. (2006, March 25). Classical conditioning and operant conditioning: Potential tools for classroom management. *Wordpress.com.* Retrieved from http://anandamahto.wordpress.com/2006/03/25/classical-conditioning-and-operant-conditioning-potential-tools-for-classroom-management/

Marshall, M. (n.d.). Retrieved September 7, 2008, from http://www.Marvin-Marshall.com

Marshall, M. (2001). *Discipline without stress punishments or rewards: How teachers and parents promote responsibility & learning.* Los Alamitos, CA: Piper Press.

Marzano, R. (2001). *Classroom instruction that works.* Denver, CO: McREL.

Marzano, R. (2007). *The art and science of teaching.* Alexandria, VA: ASCD.

Marzano, R. (2010). Using games to enhance student achievement. *Educational Leadership, 67*(5), 71–72. Retrieved from http://www.ascd.org/publications/ educational-leadership/feb10/vol67/num05/Using-Games-to-Enhance-Student-Achievement.aspx

Merryman, A. (2008). How to get kids to sleep more. *New York Magazine.* Retrieved from http://nymag.com/news/features/38979/

Michael Jordan "failure" Nike commercial. (2006, August 25). Retrieved from http:// www.youtube.com/watch?v=45mMioJ5szc&feature=related

Millman, J., & Pauk, W. (1969). *How to take tests.* New York: McGraw Hill.

Mind in the making: Essential life skills for kids. (2010, April 16). *YouTube.* Retrieved from http://www.youtube.com/watch?v=Lu1V9GM6BXE

Motive. (2001–2010). *Online etymology dictionary.* Retrieved from http://www. etymonline.com/index.php?term=motive

Neighborhood research. (2010, January 28). *Intermediate English class.* Retrieved from http://sacschoolblogs.org/burbankeld/2010/01/28/neighborhood-research/

Northwest Regional Educational Laboratory. (2004, December). *Developing self-directed learners.* Portland, OR: Author. Retrieved from http://21c-learningspecialist. wikispaces.com/file/view/Developing+Self+Directed+Learners.pdf/32329737

Ormand, C. (2008). The role of metacognition in teaching geoscience. *On the cutting edge: Professional development for geoscience faculty.* Retrieved from http://serc. carleton.edu/NAGTWorkshops/metacognition/teaching_metacognition.html

Packing your troubles away actually works, study finds. (2010, March 25). *ScienceDaily News*. Retrieved from http://www.sciencedaily.com/releases/2010/03/100324113420.htm

People who are angry pay more attention to rewards than threats. (2010, August 11). *E! Science News*. Retrieved from http://esciencenews.com/articles/2010/08/11/people.who.are.angry.pay.more.attention.rewards.threats

Perkins, D. (2003, December). Making thinking visible. *New Horizons for Learning*. Retrieved from http://www.marthalakecov.org/~building/strategies/thinking/perkins.htm

Peterson, K. D., & Stevens, D. (1988). Student reports for school teacher evaluation. *Journal of Personnel Evaluation in Education, 2*, 19–31.

Pink, D. (2009). *Drive*. New York: Riverhead Books.

Pink, D. H. (2011, January 29). Think tank: Have you ever asked yourself why you're in business? *The Telegraph*. Retrieved from http://www.telegraph.co.uk/finance/yourbusiness/8288971/Think-Tank-Have-you-ever-asked-yourself-why-youre-in-business.html

Poor children more vulnerable to effects of poor sleep. (2010, May 14). *EurekAlert!* Retrieved from http://www.eurekalert.org/pub_releases/2010–05/sfri-pcm050610.php

Poor face greater health burden than smokers or the obese. (2009, December 23). *ScienceDaily*. Retrieved from http://www.sciencedaily.com/releases/2009/12/091222141628.htm?utm_source=feedburner&utm_medium=feed&utm_campaign=Feed:+sciencedaily+(ScienceDaily:+Latest+Science+News)&utm_content=Google+Reader

Posnick-Goodwin, S. (2010, June). Cultivating resiliency in students. *California Education, 14*(9). Retrieved from http://www.cta.org/Professional-Development/Publications/Educator-June-10/Cultivating-resiliency.aspx

President Obama gives commencement address at Kalamazoo Central High School. (2010, June 7). *The White House*. Retrieved from http://www.whitehouse.gov/photos-and-video/video/president-obama-gives-commencement-address-kalamazoo-central-high-school

Prince, M., & Felder, R. (2007, March/April). The many faces of inductive teaching and learning. *Journal of College Science Teaching*. Retrieved from http://mate.calpoly.edu/media/files/Prince_Felder.pdf

Project based learning. (n.d.). Retrieved from http://pbl-online.org/faqs/faqs.htm

Project Zero. (2010). Retrieved from http://www.pz.harvard.edu/index.cfm

Q & A with Jean Twenge. (n.d.). *San Diego: San Diego State University, Department of Psychology*. Retrieved from http://www.psychology.sdsu.edu/new-web/news/TwengeQA.htm

Rathvon, N. (2008). *Effective school interventions: Evidence-based strategies for improving student outcomes*. New York: Guilford Press.

Richardson, W. (2009, February 16). Interview with Carol Dweck. *Weblogg-ed*. Retrieved from http://weblogg-ed.com/2009/interview-with-carol-dweck/

Rigoglioso, M. (2008, December). The thought of acquiring power motivates people to act. *Stanford GSB News*. Retrieved from http://www.gsb.stanford.edu/news/research/fastpower_gruenfeld.html?q=stories/the-thought-acquiring-power-motivates-people-act

Roberts, R. (2010, August 30). *Daniel Pink on drive, motivation, and incentives*. Podcast. Library of Economics and Liberty. Retrieved from http://www.econtalk.org/archives/2010/08/daniel_pink_on.html

Rodriguez, L. J. (2005). *Always running: La vida loca: Gang days in L.A.* New York: Simon and Schuster.

Rubenstein, G. (2010, August 18). News flash: How tiny boosts to personal identity improve minority students' grades. *Edutopia*. Retrieved from http://www.edutopia.org/blog/interventions-boost-esteem-academic-performance?utm_source=feedburner&utm_medium=feed&utm_campaign=Feed:+EdutopiaNew Content+(Edutopia)

Ryan, K., & Cooper, J. M. (2008). *Those who can, teach* (12th ed.). Belmont, CA: Wadsworth Publishing.

Saville, B. K. (2009, October 21). Using evidence-based teaching methods to improve education. *Teaching and Learning Excellence*. Retrieved from https://tle.wisc.edu/node/1045

Schmitt, N., & Schmitt, D. (n.d.). *Teaching vocabulary* [podcast]. Retrieved from http://www.pearsonlongman.com/professionaldevelopment/audio/podcasts/schmitts_vocab.mp3

Schwarzenegger takes responsibility for failed initiatives. (2005, November 11). *FoxNews.com*. Retrieved from http://www.foxnews.com/story/0,2933,175224,00.html

Self-control instantly replenished by self-affirmation. (2010, March 25). *Psyblog*. Retrieved from http://www.spring.org.uk/2010/03/self-control-instantly-replenished-by-self-affirmation.php?utm_source=feedburner&utm_medium=feed&utm_campaign=Feed:+PsychologyBlog+(PsyBlog)&utm_content=Google+Reader

Sheena Iyengar on the art of choosing. (2010, July). *TED*. Retrieved from http://www.ted.com/talks/sheena_iyengar_on_the_art_of_choosing.html?awesm=on.ted.com_8Tby&utm_campaign=sheena_iyengar_on_the_art_of_choosing&utm_medium=on.ted.com-twitter&utm_source=direct-on.ted.com&utm_content=ted.com-talkpage

Siegle, D. (2000). *Help students set goals*. Retrieved from http://www.gifted.uconn.edu/Siegle/SelfEfficacy/section8.html

Siegle, D. (n.d.). *Michael Jordan*. Retrieved from http://www.gifted.uconn.edu/Siegle/SelfEfficacy/Jordan.html

Sousa, D. (2006). *How the brain learns*. Thousand Oaks, CA: Corwin Press.

Sparks, S. D. (2010, December 21). Giving students a say may spur engagement and achievement. *Education Week*. Retrieved from http://blogs.edweek.org/edweek/inside-school-research/2010/12/class_choice_may_spur_student.html?utm_source=twitterfeed&utm_medium=twitter

Sparks, S. D. (2011, February 4). Study finds social-skills teaching boosts academics. *Education Week*. Retrieved from http://www.edweek.org/ew/articles/2011/02/04/20sel.h30.html?tkn=WQNFELArcqZMg0R5kEANZ%2By%2BUZUtqEboYqjH&cmp=clp-edweek

Stahl, R. J. (n.d.). Using "think-time" and "wait-time" skillfully in the classroom. *A to Z teacher stuff*. Retrieved from http://www.atozteacherstuff.com/pages/1884.shtml

Stalvey, S., & Brasell, H. (2006). Using stress balls to focus the attention of sixth-grade learners. *Journal of At-Risk Issues*, 12(2), 7–16.

Stickgold, E. (2010, May 6). School committee ok's student feedback on teachers. *The Boston Globe*. Retrieved from http://www.boston.com/news/local/massachusetts/articles/2010/05/06/school_committee_oks_student_feedback_on_teachers/

Sullo, B. (2009). *The motivated student*. Alexandria, VA: ASCD.

Sutton, B. (2008, August). It isn't just a myth: A little thanks goes a long way. *Bob Sutton: Work matters*. Retrieved from http://bobsutton.typepad.com/my_weblog/2010/08/it-isnt-just-a-myth-a-little-thanks-goes-a-long-way.html

Tangney, J. P., Baumeister, R. F., & Boone, A. L. (2004). High self-control predicts good adjustment, less pathology, better grades, and interpersonal success. *Journal of Personality*, 72(2), 271–324. Retrieved from http://onlinelibrary.wiley.com/doi/10.1111/j.0022–3506.2004.00263.x/abstract

Teens and sleep patterns. (n.d.). *5 min life videopedia*. Retrieved from http://www.5min.com/Video/Teens-and-Sleep-Patterns-143292427

The influence of positive framing. (2010, December 1). *Psyblog*. Retrieved from http://www.spring.org.uk/2010/12/the-influence-of-positive-framing.php

The standards: English language arts standards. (2010). *Common Core State Standards Initiative: Preparing America's students for college and career*. Retrieved from http://www.corestandards.org/the-standards/english-language-arts-standards

Think aloud strategy summary. (n.d.). Pebble Creek Labs. Retrieved from http://pebblecreeklabs.com/instructional-strategies/think-aloud/182-think-aloud-strategy-summary.html

Tileston, D.W. (2004). *What every teacher should know about learning, memory, and the brain*. Thousand Oaks, CA: Corwin Press.

Toppo, G. (2010, May 31). Free books block "summer slide" in low-income students. *USA Today*. Retrieved from http://www.usatoday.com/news/education/2010–06–01-summerreading01_st_N.htm

2 people can learn to cooperate intuitively, but larger groups need to communicate. (2010, November 4). *Brain Mysteries*. Retrieved from http://www.brainmysteries.com/research/2_people_can_learn_to_cooperate_intuitively_but_larger_groups_need_to_communicate.asp?utm_source=feedburner&utm_medium=feed&utm_campaign=Feed:+BrainMysteries+(Brain+News+And+Research)

U.S. Census Bureau. (2009). *Educational attainment.* Retrieved from http://www. census.gov/schools/census_for_teens/educational_attainment.html

U.S. College Search. (2010, July 19). *Unemployment applications & extension less of a concern for people with college degrees—infographic.* Retrieved from http://www. uscollegesearch.org/blog/career-planning/unemployment-applications-extension-less-of-a-concern-for-people-with-college-degrees

Van Tassell, G. (2004). Classroom management. *Brains.org.* Retrieved from http:// www.brains.org/classroom_management.htm

Viadero, D. (2010, August 16). Studies show why students study is as important as what. *Education Week.* Retrieved from http://blogs.edweek.org/edweek/ inside-school-research/2010/08/studies_show_why_students_stud.html

Viral case of the blame game. (2009, November 20). *Futurity.* Retrieved from http:// www.futurity.org/society-culture/viral-case-of-the-blame-game/

Wait time. (n.d.). *P-16 science education at the Akron Global Polymer Academy.* Retrieved from http://www.agpa.uakron.edu/p16/btp.php?id=wait-time

West Coast offense. (n.d.). *Wikipedia.* Retrieved from http://en.wikipedia.org/wiki/ West_Coast_offense

Will we succeed? The science of self-motivation. (2010, May 28). *E! Science News.* Retrieved from http://esciencenews.com/articles/2010/05/28/will.we.succeed. the.science.self.motivation

Willis, J. (2006). *Research-based strategies to ignite student learning.* Alexandria, VA: ASCD.

Willis, J. (2007). The neuroscience of joyful education. *Educational Leadership, 64.* Retrieved from http://www.district287.org/clientuploads/287Staff/SEL/ME_ PrereadingJudyWillisEdLeadArt.pdf

Wolfe, P. (2001). *Brain matters: Translating research into classroom practice.* Alexandria, VA: ASCD.

Wormeli, R. (2004). *Summarization in any subject: 50 techniques to improve student learning.* Alexandria, VA: ASCD.

Wrong way. (2008, August 31). Retrieved from http://www.youtube.com/ watch?v=CocwA5LXKlc

Yelling at students does not improve behaviour. (2010). *ACER eNews.* Retrieved from http://www.acer.edu.au/enews/2004/11/yelling-at-students-does-not-improve-behaviour

Yong, E. (2010, March 19). Requests work better than orders, even when we're asking or ordering ourselves. *Science Blogs.* Retrieved from http://scienceblogs.com/ notrocketscience/2010/03/requests_work_better_than_orders_even_when_ were_asking_or_or.php

Zadina, J. (2008). *Six weeks to a brain-compatible classroom.* Largo, FL: Author.

Zhu, E. (2010). *Practical guidelines for using technology tools in classroom teaching.* University of Michigan, Center for Research on Learning and Teaching. Retrieved from http://www.crlt.umich.edu/gsis/P4_3.php